Gifts Your Kids Can't Break

Steve&AnnieChapman

with Maureen Rank

BETHANY HOUSE PUBLISHERS
MINNEAPOLIS, MINNESOTA 55438

You may find the recordings of Steve and Annie Chapman in your
local Christian bookstore. Some of the titles include:
"No Regrets" (Cassette/CD)
"The Greatest Gift—In Concert" (Cassette/Video)
"Celebration of Womanhood" (Annie's seminar for women)
"An Evening Together—In Concert" (Double Cassette)
"The Ships Are Burning" (Cassette/CD)

Published by Bethany House Publishers
A Ministry of Bethany Fellowship, Inc.
6820 Auto Club Road, Minneapolis, Minnesota 55438

Printed in the United States of America

Library of Congress Cataloging-in-Publication Data

Chapman, Steve.
    Gifts your kids can't break / Steve and Annie Chapman with
Maureen Rank.
        p. cm.

    1. Child rearing—Religious aspects—Christianity.
2. Social values. 3. Family—Religious life.
I. Chapman, Annie. II. Rank, Maureen. III. Title.
IV. Title: Gifts your kids can not break.
HQ769.3.C45   1991
248.8'45—dc20   91–6840
ISBN 1–55661–158–7   CIP

We dedicate this book to our grandparents:

George and Easter Chapman

Ewing and Maude Steele

Eugene and Mary Williamson

Clarence and Naomi Eckard

They used their available parenting skills to shape the lives of our parents, and our parents have lovingly guided us, so that we in turn can reach out in love to our own children.

Steve & Annie

STEVE AND ANNIE CHAPMAN have been ministering to families through their music and speaking for the past ten years. They have several albums in national distribution, their music and message on the family has been featured in numerous magazines, and they perform nationwide in concerts every year. They make their home in Nashville and have two children.

MAUREEN RANK is a graduate from Iowa State University and spent six years on the Navigators staff ministering to college students. She is the author of eight books, including *Married Lovers, Married Friends, Dealing with the Dad of Your Past,* and *Free to Grieve.* She and her husband live in Knoxville, Iowa, and have two children.

Contents

1
Unbreakable Gifts

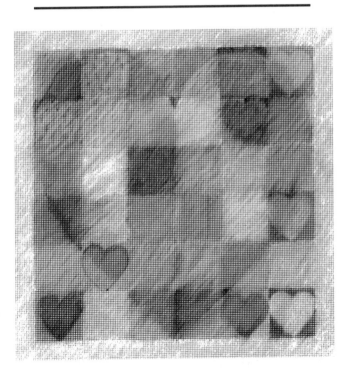

STEVE: You can count on Annie and me to be as idealistic as the next guy over the privilege of raising children to be godly adults. With all our hearts we believe Scripture when it says, "Lo, children are an heritage of the Lord" (Psalm 127:3, KJV). But there are days when child-rearing seems like anything but a privilege.

I've always enjoyed the clever song by Bill and Gloria Gaither entitled, "Kids Under Construction." After partially raising two kids of our own though, I have been inspired to write another version of that lyric, "Kids Full of Destruction."

An example is the time when Nathan, then about age four, had been out of Annie's sight for far too long. She knew it'd been too long when she heard loud crashing sounds she couldn't identify. Annie raced from the house, yelling at the top of her lungs for Nathan. When they finally met up, she found him sauntering toward the garage, dragging a ball peen hammer heavier than he was, with his chubby cheeks rounded into a satisfied grin.

I now know that if a kid is too happy about what he's just created with a ball peen hammer *you* probably won't be. My firstborn son, fruit of my loins, heir apparent to all my worldly goods, gift from heaven destined to see that the Chapman name lives on into the twenty-first century . . . this West Virginia *Wunderkind* had just taken that ball peen hammer and bashed out *all* our basement windows!

And when asked *why* on earth he'd done such an incredibly bizarre thing, he innocently replied, "Well, you never told me not to!"

And we hadn't. Rest assured, we took the opportunity to tell him then. We learned an essential parenting lesson that day. It is this: children break things, even when they don't intend to do wrong. And it isn't just male children who have potential to wreak havoc, as we later discovered.

We'd gone to New Mexico to sing, and decided this would be a good time to introduce our kids to the marvels of authentic Mexican cuisine. We found a terrific restaurant that dished out the *frijoles* and *fajitas*, and we didn't leave till the Chapman four had eaten far too *mucho*. We lumbered back to our hotel and fell into our two double beds. Heidi complained a little about her stomach, but neither Annie nor I was too concerned. Just a little South-of-the-border culture shock to a tummy raised on biscuits and gravy. She'd be fine.

We were wrong. About 1:00 A.M. Annie heard that familiar groan that can wrench any mother from the deepest sleep. Before she could act, she heard the sound of a small tummy being turned inside-out. She jumped out of bed and hastily fumbled for the light. (Realize here that Annie was sharing the bed with Heidi, so her lightning response at this point was as much from self-defense as from maternal compassion.)

Fortunately, the damage had been confined to one corner of the bed. There seemed to be enough clean area left, so Annie moved Heidi over to the clean side of the bed and then climbed in with Nathan and me.

Two more "eruptions" as the night progressed left Heidi's bed unusable. That little stomach *had* to be empty by now, we decided, so we picked up Heidi and moved her over with us in the clean bed.

But fifteen minutes later . . . you guessed it. I abandoned ship and looked for a clean section of the floor to sleep on. Nathan joined me there, and Annie tried to make do in a chair.

Morning finally came, and time to leave for the airport. We slunk away, begging the Lord to have mercy on the poor cleaning person who would have to sanitize our room. At least we hadn't been staying in someone's home as we sometimes did in those days, so were spared the humiliation of facing concert sponsors in the morning.

This thought cheered us all the way to Texas, where our concert host met us at the airport in his pride and joy—a brand-new Astro mini-van. As we pulled away from the terminal, he was halfway into a gadget-by-gadget demonstration of all the van's features, when Heidi leaned over to Annie and whispered those five fateful words, "I don't feel too good." Before we could act, the showroom perfection of that van had been destroyed forever.

Gracious man that he was, he clenched his teeth, smiled thinly, and said, "Don't worry about it." But we did. And we're wondering if he did, too, since we haven't been invited back there again!

Kids are naturally destructive, even if it's often unintentional. Breaking windows and creating messes are not uncommon occurrences. That destructive bent, however, can be disturbing when you've spent hard-earned money to purchase that "must-have" gift for Christmas, and by December 26 it's a heap of broken plastic fit for the garbage can.

But there's good news. There are gifts that will last long past Christmas. There *are* gifts that kids can't break. The gifts that we speak of are the godly values they need in order to carry them successfully through life. These gifts may even be refused or rejected for a time, but they can never be broken. Annie and I know this is true, because there were many gifts of godly character our parents tried to pass on to us. Some we accepted readily. Others we stubbornly, foolishly resisted for a time until life showed us our need of them. And still others we're turning up now, like finding treasures hidden in the attic trunks of our past.

Now we want to send our children into the world with similar solid gold values that cannot be destroyed. A wise Dutch grandmother helped us think about it in this way: When our kids go off to camp, we don't just shove them empty-handed out the door with a cheery admonition to "have a great time!" We send them off prepared by packing a suitcase filled with all the things they'll need to survive and enjoy the experience. And if we're not sure what they'll need, we compare notes with other parents and check with the camp counselors. Since we won't be with them, we want to know they're leaving us with everything they need firmly in hand for the whole time they are away.

To Annie and me, this defines parenting in a nutshell, but instead of Camp Muskeeta-bite-a as their destination, we're packing up our kids to head for *Life*. During the eighteen or twenty years they'll live under our roof, our task is to equip them with all they'll need to go on as God's people through the rest of their lives, without us constantly at their side. That means without our dollars, our direction, our discipline, *or* our devotion to God.

When Nathan or Heidi head for camp, we may forget to pack their toothbrush, or swimsuit. If we do, they'll either have to buy it at the camp store, or make do without it. But in packing for Life, forgetting to instill an essential godly quality can have devastating consequences. Not knowing how to handle money can lead to financial ruin. Not being able to establish a loving relationship can bring them to divorce. Not discovering God for themselves can leave them spiritually empty and lost.

When Nathan was a toddler, Annie busily set about trying to do everything for him. Fortunately, a wise mother of seven recognized Annie's misguided "smother-love". "Annie," she said, "your goal as a mother should be to work yourself out of a job. For instance, if your son can't cross a busy street alone by the time he's six years old, you're failing as a mother." Her challenge redirected us. Instead of trying to protect our kids from struggles, we began to see parenting as preparing them to meet struggles with wisdom and courage.

Scripture pictures it this way: "We are God's children. Now if we are children, then we are heirs—

heirs of God and co-heirs with Christ" (Romans
8:16, 17). Right now, Annie and I are responsible to
administer the riches God has left us in Christ.
Later, it'll be Nathan and Heidi's turn to act as ad-
ministrators of God's estate. We need to help ready
them to manage wisely by giving them gifts that
can't be broken.

To prepare them, we've taken as our guide this
challenge from God:

> Fix these words of mine in your hearts and
> minds . . . teach them to your children, talking
> about them when you sit at home and when
> you walk along the road, when you lie down
> and when you get up . . . so that your days
> and the days of your children may be many in
> the land that the Lord swore to give your fore-
> fathers. (Deuteronomy 11:18–21)

If this sounds like an overwhelming challenge, believe me—we know how you feel. We
weren't always sold on the value of godly parenting.

In fact, when we were first married, Annie
wasn't enthusiastic about the idea of having children. She made it known that, to her, kids would
be an intrusion on an otherwise blissful life. She
had dreams and ambitions, and didn't see how
children fit into the lifestyle she envisioned for
us. I hadn't given it much thought one way or
the other, so her convictions seemed reasonable
enough at the time.

But one weekend not long after our first an-
niversary, we drove back to my hometown of

Chapmanville, West Virginia. (Yes, I really did grow up in a town called Chapmanville, named after distant relatives.) We'd gone home for my grandfather's funeral. Grandpa Chapman and his wife Easter had eleven children—eight sons and three daughters. So, crammed into that little funeral parlor were dozens and dozens of people who were first-, second-, and third-generation offspring of what began as just two.

Later that evening as we drove home, Annie now tells me, she reflected quietly on how many people had come from that one man and his wife. And it occurred to her that because of these offspring, Grandpa would never die, in a way, for he would live on in his children and his children's children. At that moment, the Lord seemed to drop this thought into her mind: "Steve is an honorable man. I want what he stands for to live on, as well."

With that apparent directive from God, Annie had to reconsider her decision about childbearing. Perhaps parenting meant more than filling up our lives with diaper-changing and redecorating our home in "early Fisher-Price." Maybe parenting actually had more to do with *heir*-raising—extending the positive influence of our lives—and more importantly, of God's life through raising children.

We discovered that this is exactly what God wants. Having children is not just something we do to possess an "ideal family" (2.5 children, a dog, and a cat) or to feel complete as adults—it is *for Him*. As Malachi tells us, God made man and woman one flesh in the covenant of marriage "because He was seeking godly offspring" (Malachi 2:15).

Once we'd gotten this new perspective on parenting, a pregnancy soon followed.

Personally, I threw myself enthusiastically into the fathering role. My first official "father" act was to gain forty pounds during the pregnancy, topping Annie's weight gain. I figured I was eating for three!

I showed equal enthusiasm for the Lamaze classes in natural childbirth which we attended. There they told us how breathing heavily could greatly ease the trauma of childbirth and I took them seriously. While Annie delivered the baby, I actually hyperventilated. The Lamaze people were absolutely right about their breathing idea, though. I sailed through the delivery without feeling a thing!

Other parts of parenting I didn't take to quite as naturally. I recall the first time Annie left the house and I wound up caring for Nathan all alone. Our baby was barely two weeks old and friends had invited Annie to go strawberry picking. Since she'd hardly left our baby's side for fourteen days straight, she jumped at the chance. As she left, she cooed, "Honey, if the baby needs changing, you'll have to change him."

Not being astute at infant care, I hoped that when Annie said "change the baby," she meant something comparatively easier than re-diapering—like changing his personality. But he seemed fine to me. So I set out to do what I planned to do that afternoon, which was to work on a song. While the lyrics were flowing, though, so was my son's plumbing. Annie came home to a soggy, howling child. (In my defense, I said I was *just* ready to go check on him when she walked in the door.) You'd have thought I'd sold him to a passing band of gypsies by the nasty look Annie shot at me. And I deserved it. I had a lot to learn, to put it mildly.

But I *am* learning, and Annie is too, right along with me. And the most important things we're learning go far beyond the mechanics of diaper-changing, bike repair, and training in table manners. We're learning to view these two children as future soldiers in God's army, future heirs of the values we hold most dear.

One thing I want to make clear: We are not child-rearing experts. We're not interested in duplicating the scene Annie witnessed after church one day as she visited with two other mothers. One was the mother of beautiful children who were able to dress themselves, feed themselves, and go to the bathroom on their own. They were teenagers. The first listened as the second woman—parent of a toddler and a colicky new-born—told about her exhaustion after enduring weeks of her baby's relentless crying.

The mother of the teenagers, looking tanned and well-rested, looked into the young mother's bloodshot eyes and said with all sincerity, "But you must remember that these are the *best* days of your life."

Annie thought she was about to witness a

homicide right there on the sidewalk.

Now when I sing our songs about making the most of every minute with our precious children, I shudder to think of some poor listening father in the past, whose sixteen-year-old just came home sporting pink hair and a black leather mini-skirt. I imagine that dad would like to have choked me! Having our children get older has helped us to see that what works for a three-year-old won't necessarily work for a kid of thirteen.

Our pastor-friend Bob Russell tells of the young minister who confidently created a series of sermons entitled "The Ten Commandments for Raising Children."

After he'd had a child or two, however, the series shortened down to "Five Suggestions for Guiding Children."

By the time his kids were teenagers, the sermon title read, "A Couple of Hints for Being a Successful Parent."

Now he's a grandfather, and on the rare occasions he can be coerced to speak to parents, he calls his talk, "Mom and Dad—Good Luck!"

As parents, Annie and I are somewhere between "The Ten Commandments" and "Good Luck!" And on days we think we know it all, we remember the father of twelve we met after a concert. He told us he laughs when he sees books on raising kids. After a dozen kids, 57 grandkids, and 17 great-grandkids, he's decided there's no pat formula. Each child is different enough to warrant a book of his own.

However, we do believe God hasn't left us to

muddle through by trial and error. He intends that we have a game plan to follow. People without a plan in any part of life operate at a disadvantage.

Consider the poor guy with no long-range financial plan trying to manage his money. He's the one holding his breath from crisis to crisis, hoping it'll all come out alright in the end. You'll find him scrambling around at 11:30 P.M. to find a grocery store that will cash a check so he can finance the family outing to Adventure World the next day. Then the day after, he's off to the bank to clear up "insufficient funds" charges because he's overdrawn his account. It isn't that he doesn't have money—it's just that the money isn't where he needs it because he's given it no forethought. We can get caught in a similar trap as parents if we don't work out a long-range strategy for parenting.

Therefore, a godly strategy must include deciding on the gifts our kids are going to need to make it without us, and then finding ways to equip them with those things. Annie and I have chosen eleven values to share with you that we are working on with Nathan and Heidi. We share them not as final answers, but as ideas to encourage you to develop your own strategy for equipping your children for life.

As the bedrock for all else that we'll share, the first value or gift is one that we believe is foundational to a child's godly character—a sense of importance.

2

Importance

STEVE: Everybody wants to be the MVP—Most Valuable Player. But most of us are just PAG's—Pretty Average Guys—trying to figure out how to be important in an MVP world.

It matters that we find a way to be important, and it matters that our kids do, as well. If we can equip them with a sense that they are Somebody, we've given them a solid footing for the day when they'll have to stand on their own.

I recall a Christian family that grew up down the road from us back in West Virginia. The kids were taken to church, subjected to family devotions, and taught biblical principles. But they were also taught that humility meant everyone else was always *more* important than they were. Everyone else was a Somebody; they were to be Nobodies for Jesus' sake. Noble as this teaching may sound to some, it did not produce rugged soldiers of the Cross in this family. Instead, each of the five children went on to marry spouses whose moral values were decidedly lower than theirs. I can't help but wonder if these children felt they couldn't expect a Somebody to marry a Nobody, so they settled for mates with a weaker character.

It's true that Scripture commands us to "humbly

treat others as better than yourselves." But it also goes on to explain, "Each of you be interested *not only* in your own things, *but also* in those of others." (Philippians 2:3, 4, Beck, emphasis mine.) The Lord doesn't want us to ignore others' needs and opinions, but neither does He intend that we ignore or devalue our own.

Annie's family, the Williamsons, had a clear understanding about teaching kids to feel important. For instance, the Williamsons were in the minority as Republicans in what seemed to be a whole county of Democrats. Their stance was not an easy one to maintain, but Annie's parents didn't waiver. They told their kids, "On this Republican issue, we believe we're right. So if no one else agrees, they must all be wrong!"

I, on the other hand, grew up in a family so entrenched in the Democratic Party that voting for Eisenhower was like committing the unpardonable sin. I remember my grandaddy holding up his little finger and declaring, "If there was even an ounce of Republican blood in this finger I'd cut it off up to my elbow!" Statements like this made me aware there must be Republicans in the world, but I wasn't interested in meeting any. You can imagine the "creative tension" this generated for Annie and me when it turned out I'd married one!

Though Annie at times has had to rethink her family's political convictions, there is one conviction she held on to. *Even if most people don't agree with her, that doesn't make her wrong.* Other people may be Somebodies, but she is a Somebody, too, and her convictions matter just as much as theirs. That's the kind of godly self-importance that will equip our children to be strong and true to good values and moral uprightness.

Valuing themselves will also free them from trying to be somebody they aren't. When Scripture challenges us as parents to "train up a child in the way he should go," it's not just talking about teaching the general path of godliness. The verse emphasizes each child as an individual, uniquely equipped with a particular mix of strengths and weaknesses, abilities and needs. The Lord wants our kids to appreciate and use their own unique qualities to their fullest, and if they value themselves that's just what they'll do.

Heidi and Nathan aren't alike in much of anything. For instance, connect Nathan to an object with wheels, turn him outside to go as hard and as fast and as long as he can, and he's in glee. Heidi, however, was born without the capacity to even mention the word "sweat." Her idea of a good time is two hours alone in her room with 168 stuffed animals and a stack of books. The two children simply are not alike, and the same things don't get their juices going. Even though we encourage Nathan to read and Heidi to get physical exercise, we need to recognize their individual uniqueness and make allowances for them.

When we parents rightly teach our kids their unique value, that confidence will stay with them their whole lives. Annie doesn't mind my sharing the fact that she was quite overweight as a child. Her older sister, on the other hand, was pencil-slim and striking enough to enter local beauty pageants.

But Annie never remembers her parents mentioning her weight, acting ashamed of her, or comparing her unfavorably to her sister. Annie says, "My dad thought I was beautiful." They praised what she did well, which was helping outdoors with the farm chores, and singing. Because they valued Annie as *Annie*, with her unique qualities and talents, I now have the privilege of sharing life with a woman who works hard enough for five people and warms the lives of thousands with her songs.

My dad showed the same wisdom. I was born with a passion to hunt and fish. In my estimation, a life spent tramping through the biggest, darkest, thickest woods around would be a life worth living. Annie tells people I have an incurable case of that rare disease JJS—Jeremiah Johnson Syndrome—and she could be right.

But my dad had no such interest. He's now in his sixties, and to my knowledge, he spent not a day of his adult years hunting or fishing. But he never belittled my interest. He encouraged me to connect with another man in our church who loved the outdoors as much as I did. And he willingly shared my time and admiration with this man named Kenneth Bledsoe, who taught me about hunting and fishing. Now that I have a son of my own I realize what a generous gift that actually was.

Because my dad recognized my interest in the sport and gave me the freedom to pursue it, I now have a way to relax that completely recharges my batteries. If the songs aren't coming, a day in the woods will usually spark them again. But had my dad not valued the essential part of me that needs to be alone—even though it wasn't part of him—I might never have accepted it myself.

A while back, our family was working on a song we would soon need to perform in the recording studio. Each of the kids was to sing a solo verse, then sing a verse in unison, followed by Annie and me singing lines alternately. We would then finish up singing together. The song went fine until we tried the last part. The four of us singing in unison sounded terrible!

I should have expected problems, because it normally takes months of vocal training for a small group to sing successfully in unison. We were going to need another approach. I noticed that the kids sang fine together when it was just the two of them, but adding the adult voices made their sense of pitch go haywire.

"Let's try this," I suggested. "On the last bar, you sing alto, Annie, and I'll take the tenor." When we hit the chord in harmony, we both knew there had to be angels in the room—but lo, it was only us! The kids weren't impressed, but Mom and Dad were. We made them do it again and again until they begged to stop.

I've thought often about that day, because it says something to me about encouraging our uniqueness. Our family doesn't produce beauty when we are forced to be all alike. Harmonious singing—and harmonious living—requires that we be different from each other. It is my prayer that the Lord will help us to value our differences and allow them to blend into something of beauty.

When you value something, tell your children how important it is.

A woman in Alabama told us about being with her husband at his father's deathbed. As the end approached, the father suddenly sat upright with a look of terror on his face. "What's happening to me, Son?" he cried, grasping for the younger man, and then he sank back into the pillows.

The woman's husband was so visibly shaken, he staggered out into the hall. Joining him, the wife said softly, "This must be so terrible for you to have seen your dad dying this way."

"That's not what got to me," her husband choked out. "It's that this is the first time in my life he ever called me 'Son'."

The moment of my death will *not* be the first time my children hear how much they mean to me. I've seen to that. Jesus didn't wait until the Cross to let His disciples know how much He valued them. When He first met Nathaniel He said, "Here is a true Israelite, in whom there is nothing false." And after a year or so with Simon He said, "Blessed are you, Simon, son of Jonah . . . and I tell you that you are Peter—the Rock." The Gospels radiate with His affirmations toward these and the rest of His disciples.

When Nathan celebrated his thirteenth birthday, Annie asked me to write a letter to him to mark the occasion, telling him how I felt about his passage into manhood. There was only one thing wrong with this idea—I wished I'd thought of it first! But for those of us who don't find it easy to express to our kids how much we value them, a bit of prodding is sometimes in order. So I set pen to paper and this is what I came up with:

Dear Nathan,

It's March 1990. We're on another airplane, en route to Chicago (or somewhere). I hate to fly, you know that, (and you're not too fond of it, either). But today there's a distraction. We're not thinking too much about traveling, we're thinking about Tuesday . . . the celebration of your birthday. Not just any birthday. It's #13! You will officially be a "teenager." A certified, order-from-the-adult-menu teenager!

You've heard us do our concert many times. And you've heard us say things about teenagers. Usually when we refer to teenagers, it's followed by a "Shall we pray?" Then everyone laughs. Why? Because it can be such a tough time for everyone.

But we do not hate this day. If there's a reason to feel at all uneasy, it's only because it represents a turning point that is sobering for you and me and for all of us. This Tuesday reminds us we can't stop time. It keeps plowing through our lives. This day forces us to face a hard fact. You *are* indeed growing up.

After Tuesday, we will think differently about you. You will think differently, too. There's *something* about becoming a teenager.

With all the changes ahead for you and for us we'll pray for you as they "hit." But we also pray that you'll never change in some ways. We hope you'll always be as sensitive to right and wrong as you have been. Also, we hope you'll always be in awe, absolute awe, of the God who made us and loves us and takes care of us through Jesus Christ.

Finally, may you always be as kind to others as you are to us (and me especially). When you put your hand on my shoulder and say "Dad, I love you!" I am deeply touched. Your words feel like warm sunshine on those cold deer-hunting mornings. Your words taste better than that 5th Avenue candy bar at 10:00 A.M. on those squirrel-season mornings. Those words echo through time and into eternity where God lives, and they touch His heart, too!

I love you, Nathan. And I will love you all the Tuesdays ahead, no matter how many you'll have.

With all my heart,
Dad

When you value something, don't just say it's important— back up your words with actions.

Listen to the observations of Dr. Scott Peck, a psychiatrist who has been involved with thousands of troubled people:

Some basically unloving parents, in an attempt to cover up their lack of caring, make frequent professions of love to their children, repetitively and mechanically telling them how much they are valued, but not devoting significant time of high quality to them. Their children are never totally deceived by such hollow words. Consciously they may cling to them, wanting to believe that they are loved, but unconsciously they know that their parents' words do not match up with their deeds.

The time and quality of the time that their parents devote to them indicate to children the degree to which they are valued by their parents.[1]

Whew! What I decide to do with my *time* may speak more loudly to my kids than my words. My actions tell them, "You are important." And even better—"You are more important than . . ." Than what? Than the song I'm working on right now? Than my afternoon of golf? Than my friends' opinions of me? Than the TV? Or money?

Maybe these decisions about giving your kids time are easy for you. They aren't for me. I love parenting, but life consists of more than parenting. And my responsibilities, commitments and dreams pull at me from a thousand different directions, fuzzing up the issue of time for the kids.

Like the time a couple of years ago when Annie and I were invited to a prestigious Christian music conference. We were to talk to the Christian musicians there about balancing family needs and ministry demands. On top of that, we were offered the chance to do a concert with some Gospel Music "greats." What an opportunity! Here in just a few short sessions we might have the chance to make an impact for the family that would take years for us to make otherwise. We

---

[1]M. Scott Peck, M.D. , *The Road Less Traveled* (New York: Simon and Schuster, 1978), pp. 23, 24.

had a chance to influence the *influencers*, and to be on stage with "the biggies."

But blam! Our balloon popped when we realized the conference was scheduled for the first week in August. August—the four weeks out of that year we'd already committed to our children as Family Weeks. Our children travel with us in our music ministry, so this "carrot" of taking August off had kept them going through a hectic year on the road. And with an equally pressured schedule beginning in September, there was no way to reschedule our time away.

I struggled over this one. Helping these musicians give their families top priority might mean indirectly helping all those they ministered to. And I'll admit it honestly: It also occurred to me that it wouldn't hurt our professional advancement, either, to be featured at this convention.

It didn't take hours in prayer to understand God's perspective. How ridiculous to think I could justify putting my family's needs second so that we could fly off to Colorado and tell others how they needed to put their families first! Even now as I say it, I can hear how silly it sounds, but at the time—with thoughts of influence and esteem filling up my head—it made some sense.

Some of our "time-with-the-kids" decisions are big ones, like the one I've just described. But the more important ones are small—judgment calls about the seconds and minutes of ordinary Thursday mornings and uneventful Monday nights. Like when I'm headed to the mall—will I ask Heidi if she wants to ride along and then *talk* to her about her concerns instead of listening to the ball game on the radio? Or when Nathan needs help again to remember the chores he's responsible for—will I stick with him until they're done or let it slide by because I don't want to take the time? The gift of giving time is even more precious than giving words.

There are also actions that serve better than others to instill in our kids a sense of importance and worth. In his excellent book *How to Really Love Your Child*, Dr. Ross Campbell explains three simple techniques that can make all the difference in your child's *feeling* that you value him: eye contact, physical contact, and focused attention.

They work like this: When you have something positive to say to your child, get down on his level, put your hand on his shoulder, look straight into his eyes, then give him your words of love. Dr. Campbell reminds parents that we too often use eye contact and physical contact only when we scold or correct our kids, so the power of these tools are used only to make a negative impact.

When kids are small, opportunities for physical contact come more easily. But as they grow, they can be out the door before we even see them. It's possible to go all day without once touching or kissing them, and yet older kids need physical reassurance as much as little ones do.

Then, Dr. Campbell says, we need to listen with focused attention. The next time your kid runs in with a "Hey, Mom," or "Hey, Dad," *stop* what you are doing. Take time to focus on them.

Make eye contact. And *listen*. A dose of physical contact here—a pat on the back, a squeeze on the arm—emphasizes the fact that you are indeed listening and care about what they're saying. You are affirming in the most powerful way possible, "You *matter*. Nothing in the world is as important to me right now as what you have to say."

Teach kids their value, even when they hurt you.

It had been one of our busiest Septembers ever. I had about three minutes off one afternoon, so I decided to dig out my golf clubs and head for the backyard to try a few swings. (I'll admit it, I'm hooked on golf, though I'm not proud of my compulsion about it. A golf widow I know believes that Satan's temptation in Eden didn't involve an apple at all. According to her, the serpent crooned, "Adam . . . I've got the golf clubs, Adam. Accurate putter. Lengthy woods. You can play every Sunday, Adam.")

Be that as it may, I had just gotten started, when Heidi spotted me and asked if she could try. I handed her my five-iron and let her take a swing. As it turned out, she had a beautiful, natural swing and visions of my daughter as the next Nancy Lopez flashed through my brain. Also the word "scholarships" came with debt-free rush! With just a little instruction, maybe . . .

"Heidi, let me help you," I offered. "I can teach you everything I know—and it will only take a minute."

I turned her around with her back toward me, and put my hand on her head so I could tilt it down toward the ball.

"Now, Heidi, a good golf swing means you keep your head down and your eyes on the ball so the club will take the same path every time you swing it. Now try that."

That's the last thing I remember.

What I had failed to tell her was to be sure no one was in the way of her swing. So my blossoming young golfer swung and smacked her old dad right in the face!

Eight stitches and, by Heidi's estimation, about three gallons of blood later, things had quieted down. But that episode gave me the chance to hold her and comfort her as she cried. And it gave me a moment to grace her with my forgiveness.

I came away with a scar. But I'm not sorry, because it reminds her that even when we hurt each other she will always be mine. That scar has also blessed me as well, because it reminds me I value my children—and I have the scars to prove it! After all, the One to whom I belong values *me*, and has much more costly scars to prove His love.

Teach kids their ultimate value.

Finally, I know I must teach my children that their worth is ultimately found in only one place. They must realize who they are in Jesus Christ.

My dad passed this on to me in a unique way. When I'd leave the house for school or to go to a ball game or the Dairy Queen, he would *always* say, "Remember whose child you are!"

Later, during my time in the Navy, I chose not to follow the Lord. But one day on an aircraft carrier in the middle of the Mediterranean Dad's words came back to me. Suddenly, I understood what he'd really been saying all those years. The message was, "Steve, you are a child of God. You have royal blood. Your Father is the maker of the universe—the Father of Abraham, Isaac and Jacob. You are His child, so remember whose child you are."

On that day, I began to turn back toward Christ. If our children are truly going to know their importance they too must be taught—by words and actions—whose children they are.

3

Encouragement

ANNIE: As if it were happening at this moment, I can close my eyes and recall my father taking my little-girl chin in his hand, looking me straight in the eye and saying, "Annie, I can tell by the look in your eye you can do *anything* you want to do."

At that instant, if they'd been taking applicants for the next space mission I'd have marched right over and signed up. If Bert Parks had been ready to announce the next Miss America, I'd have wrestled the microphone from him and announced that *I* was the one to wear the crown. My dad's few words were affirmation, inspiration and motivation for me.

But if a little is good, does it follow that more is necessarily better?

A few weeks ago I tried unsuccessfully to gulp scalding coffee from a mug we'd picked up in our travels, so while the coffee cooled, I decided to read the mug. (I have so little time to read that my exposure to great literature has sunk to this abysmal level, though I doubt I'm much different than most Americans. Why doesn't someone publish *War and Peace* on bumper stickers or T-shirts? I might get through it then.)

Anyway, the mug I'd selected from my library of literary greats was entitled "102 Ways to Praise Your Child." It began innocently enough. "Nice job," "We like having you live here," "Since you cleaned under your bed I no longer worry about alien life forms growing there." Things like that.

But as I progressed around the mug, the praises became more and more extravagant. "You are fantastic," "Positively 100 percent!" "You're incredible," "Nothing can stop you," "You're spectacular," "Phenomenal"—and my personal favorite—"You are perfect."

This mug was describing kids? How far would the praises go? Would #102 be, "Western civilization couldn't survive without you?"

I thought back to that bit of encouragement from my dad. Now it sounded a bit flat compared to some of these verbal extravaganzas. What if Dad had flowered up his words and added 101 other phrases to it? Would I have been 101 times happier, or achieved 101 times more than I have? I wondered.

Not long after that, a friend told me about being with her son at the funeral home as they grieved her father's death. As she received the condolences of friends, she noticed her son standing alone at the back of the funeral home, crying. Assuming he was overwhelmed with grief, she hurried to console him. But she found he wasn't weeping over the loss of his grandfather at all. He was upset because attending this wake meant he was going to miss his Little League game!

The mother told me later, "I realized then, we

have given this child too much."

Of course it's not fair to judge one's whole character on the basis of one selfish response. And I know experts remind us that children don't always express grief directly. But when I heard this mother's assessment, I wondered again . . .

Could it be we've gone overboard with praise?

It's possible. Dr. Ralph Minear, of the pediatrics department at Harvard Medical School, thinks we modern parents have gone overboard with most everything else. In his book *Kids Who Have Too Much*, he warns, "A social epidemic is endangering the physical and emotional health of our country's children. 'Affluenza,' the Rich Kids Syndrome, attacks not only the children of the wealthy but also those of middle-class and low-income families. Parents are pressuring their children into becoming overachievers while giving them excessive amounts of freedom, money, food, information and protection."[1]

Perhaps finding 102 ways to praise your child is too much, as well.

But is there a way to affirm our children without overdosing them on overblown accolades? I dearly hope so, and to that end Steve and I are working on giving our children what we call "reality-based encouragement," and in learning to do it we've agreed on five "don'ts" to guide us.

---

[1]Dr. Ralph E. Minear and William Proctor, *Kids Who Have Too Much* (Nashville: Thomas Nelson Publishers, 1989), from the dust jacket.

One:
Don't praise the kids for routinely taking care of the everyday necessities of life.

A child-rearing book of a decade ago pushed a principle called "Catch 'em being good." The idea was this: Instead of always snipping at the children for their naughtiness, simply wait until they do something right—being quiet, picking up a toy, carrying a shirt to the hamper—and praise them for it. If we did this consistently, the author claimed our wee ones' little self-esteems would blossom. Gradually the beautiful flowers of good behavior would crowd out the ugly weeds of bad behavior. They'd be motivated to be good for the reward of our praise.

What could be wrong with that?

For one thing, this philosophy isn't scriptural. The Bible teaches that every person since Adam is born with or has a bent toward a sinful nature. All the encouragement in the world won't weed out the rebellion within us.

A Kansas City mother showed me a second flaw in this philosophy. Her children's school built their discipline around this "catch 'em being good" idea. Nearly every time her children did anything that wasn't bad they were given a piece of candy. Completing a routine assignment merited candy. Not causing trouble on the playground brought candy. It was almost to the point where she wondered if simply showing up for school with their clothes on would earn them candy!

The problem is, life doesn't work this way. My friend says, "No one welcomes me out of bed in the morning with a 'Good for you, Norma!' When I fix breakfast for my children, no one stands at the stove with a $10 bill to reward me. When my husband changes a flat tire on the car, he won't be given a box of chocolates for his good deed. Much of life consists of simply doing what has to be done because it *has* to be done. Continual reinforcement for accepting normal responsibilities teaches our kids to expect praise for everything. They may become responsible only when they're praised for it, and that's an unrealistic expectation."

Her convictions helped assuage my guilt about the mornings we have to pull the kids out of bed at 4:00 or 5:00 A.M. to catch an early flight to a concert. It occurred to me that my father would occasionally awaken me at 5:00 A.M. to look for a cow that might be calving. If I didn't find her, we might lose the calf *and* a chunk of our income for the year.

But my father didn't send me a handwritten thank-you note every time he woke me early. I understood it to be my duty as part of the family. It reminds me of a parable Jesus told about a servant who'd been working all day, and then was expected to prepare the master's supper before he could sit down himself to eat. Jesus asked, "Would he [the master] thank the servant because he did what he was told to do? So you also, when you have done everything you were told to do, should say, 'We are unworthy servants; we have only done our duty' " (Luke 17:9, 10).

Of course the first time Heidi made her own bed, she deserved warm praise, and she got it. And as she began to develop a pattern of consistency she was praised. But does a ten-year-old need daily praise for simply making her bed? We don't think so.

Two:
Don't praise the kids in extravagant terms for average achievements.

Remember my "102 Ways" mug? What sort of accomplishment should earn the response: "*Absolutely phenomenal!*" Should it be given to an 8-year-old for emptying the trash when this has been his assigned weekly job for nearly a year? I doubt it.

When we praise kids so lavishly for good, but not extraordinary performance, we're teaching them that putting forth very little effort should reap enormous returns. We all know the scripture that warns us to not think more highly of ourselves than we ought. Doesn't overly extravagant praise invite our children to do just that?

And it makes our words mean nothing when we praise them for doing the truly remarkable. Our language, after all, has only so many superlatives. So what do you say when your 8-year-old trash emptier makes an effort that *for him* is truly fantastic—say, when he chooses not to be controlled by his terror of deep water and cannonballs off the diving board? When we shout, "Fantastic!"—so what? Doing his weekly chores rated a "fantastic." Is this step of maturity no better than taking out trash?

Three:
You don't have to provide opportunities for your kids to do everything.

Because our children go with us on the road, Nathan has never had the chance to play Little League baseball. Steve and I have felt guilty about this. Sports were one of Steve's great pleasures of growing up. So when we'd drive by a baseball field full of rambunctious little boys, on our way to the airport *again*, pangs of remorse would stab Steve. Surely he was depriving our son of an integral pleasure of childhood by insisting he be part of our vagabond lifestyle.

One day it came to me how ridiculous this was. It was true, Nathan didn't play Little League or soccer. But we had provided chances for alternative sports that didn't require a team, like golf, biking and hunting. And consider the experiences he was having while other boys played Little League! By thirteen, he'd already seen most of the United States. He'd already had the chance to work side by side with his father in the family business. And he'd been exposed to some of the most wonderful people of God. Does a child need to do everything—or even the *same* things as his peers?

Unfortunately, many of the people I know would say yes. The message permeating our thinking today seems to be, "Have it all. Do it all.

Be all." Like the kid's T-shirt I saw last Christmas put it, "Dear Santa, I want everything!"

Harvard pediatrician, Ralph Minear, says, "In themselves, material things and other seeming advantages that children have aren't bad or undesirable. On the contrary, rightly used, they can get a youngster off to a fast, effective start in realizing his full potential in life. But sometimes it's possible to get too much of a good thing, to get good things in the wrong way, or to receive 'advantages' with the wrong messages attached."[2]

One or two sports may be fine, three may constitute "too much of a good thing." Piano lessons may develop your child beautifully, but will piano *and* flute *and* ballet *and* the library reading program do four times as much?

After a magazine article challenged parents to spend more time with their children, one angry mother wrote, "You've got to let up on this 'time with the kids' guilt-trip! My husband and I just can't do more, because our work demands such long hours. And we must work these hours because there's no way to make it financially otherwise. After all, should I have to tell my son he can't play field hockey because we can't afford the expensive equipment and shoes?"

Her frustrated response makes me want to ask some questions. Is field hockey the only sport her son plays? Is it the only extra activity or class or camp in which he wants to be involved? If it is, and his parents can't afford it without endless

---

[2]Minear, pp. 11, 12.

hours of work, then they have my sympathy, indeed.

But what if field hockey is simply *one more* activity in a list of sports and hobbies he participates in. Having to forego field hockey might actually be best for this child. Many sane, productive people have made it to adulthood without knowing a field hockey stick from a stick of Juicy Fruit. The *gluttony of activity* can be as harmful, I believe, as food gluttony.

Four:
Don't console the kids when what they need is challenge.

When Heidi was six, she decided she wanted to ride a bike. I took her bike out of the garage and positioned her on the seat. Then I started pushing while she pedaled. Off we went, her little legs pumping as I held up the bike. I planned to steady her until she got the feel of it—then I'd let go and watch her sail away.

After one attempt at this, however, Heidi realized my letting go could mean she might wreck. So the next time I started to let go, she slammed on the brakes, jarring my entire spine enough to qualify me as a chiropractic emergency.

Model Mother that I am, I choked back my pain and said sweetly, "Now, Heidi. You don't want to put on the brakes like that. When I let go, you want to keep right on pedaling."

Of course she didn't *want* to keep right on pedaling, so the next time I lightened my grip—

screech! She slammed to a stop again, and once again I was shaken badly enough to loosen fillings.

We'd set a pattern here. I'd push, Heidi would pump, I'd begin to let go, Heidi would brake. "Look, Heidi, don't you want to learn to ride a bike?" I asked through clenched teeth.

"No, I don't," she said. "I just want to *ride* a bike. I never said anything about wanting to *learn*."

At least the child was honest.

After a few days of this, I'd had my fill. So one bright Tuesday, I announced, "Heidi, today you are going to ride your bike on your own or else!"

What did I mean? Actually, I thought that *I* couldn't take another session of those unnerving jolts. But I didn't tell her that, and I dragged her outside to her bicycle.

The scene was as bad as you can imagine. I'd start pushing, and she'd slam on the brakes and fall. "You get up and try it again!" I'd say. The next time she'd go a foot or two solo. Then wreck. But as she lay there squalling, I'd yell, "*You get up!*" (Heidi may one day write a book about this experience and title it *Annie Dearest*. . . .)

But before the day was over, Heidi finally decided I meant what I said. Since she had no choice in the matter, she let herself stop screaming long enough to get the feel of balancing. And at long last, she held upright and kept on going. Hey!— this was fun! "Hey, Mom, I'm riding my bike!"

she called. You'd have thought she *invented* bicycling.

I managed a weak wave at her as she wheeled off to show the neighbor kids, then staggered into the house.

To console her for her fears of biking might have made Heidi feel good, and certainly would have made her feel warmer toward me. But that consolation might have kept her from doing what in the end made her feel a thousand times better. She faced what she feared, and overcame it. And without my challenging her, she might still be bound by an unnecessary fear. (Plus, she might have wound up the only 65-year-old woman in Nashville with her mother still pushing her around on her bike!)

I have found that I need not fear the struggle my kids go through as they grow and learn. It's the struggle that makes them strong enough to survive. Back on the farm in West Virginia, we hatched baby chicks each spring. I'd see those peepers fighting to peck their way out of the shell and my heart would melt. So to help the tiny things, I decided to peel away the shell for them. To my disappointment, each chick I "helped" in this way soon died. I didn't know they were developing the strength they needed to survive during that struggle to free themselves from the eggshell. When I denied them the struggle, I robbed them of the stamina they needed to live in the outside world. My kindness killed them!

How easy it would be to make the same mistake with Heidi and Nathan. We can start by letting them learn as babies to go to sleep without having to be rocked every night (even if learning demands some nights of crying it out). And we can keep on right through adolescence by letting them live with the painful consequences of missed opportunities or bad decisions.

When kids need consolation, let's give it. But let's not coddle them when they need challenge.

Five:
Don't take responsibility for things that aren't a parent's responsibility.

You know the scenario: The history test is tomorrow, and your seventh grader hasn't studied enough. The Cubs game is on TV, the neighbor kid wants him to come skateboard, and he hasn't gotten to play Super Mario Brothers for days.

Loud moan here, followed by chest-deep sigh. "*Why* do I have to know this history stuff anyway? Grown-ups don't even know this stuff, and they get along fine." Then the child peers at you. "Okay, I'll prove it. You tell me, who was the most important emperor of Rome in the second century?"

As you may have guessed, that scene came straight from Nathan's last history study session.

But when he hit me with the emperor of Rome question, I stared right back. "Nathan, I do not need to know who ruled Rome in the second century. School is *your* job. I have a job *I'm* responsible for. So get to studying."

Awhile back I heard a psychiatrist analyzing

the families of alcoholics. He said, "Often, it's more important to the parents that their son or daughter be sober than it is to the child. But until the child cares, he'll never be sober, and the power struggle to *make* him care will tear the family apart."

When our children are small, we carry enormous responsibility for them. But as they grow, we must turn over to them, one by one, responsibilities that are rightly theirs. They may not carry them as well as we did, and they may even fail sometimes. But if they are to be our heirs, they're going to inherit adult responsibilities as well as adult privileges.

How much more acceptable it is for them if we allow them to inherit those responsibilities a little at a time, not dumping them on them all at once when they are out of our house for good! And how comforting if we strengthen them to carry those responsibilities, cheering them on with encouragement that's based in reality.

4

Work and Money

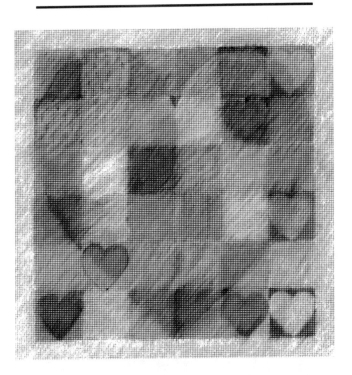

STEVE: Poor Annie! It wasn't until she was in college that she learned the truth about Labor Day. At her house, that September day meant rolling out the wheelbarrow, washing out the paint brushes and slapping a fresh coat of white paint over everything on the farm that didn't move. (This included, I'm told, any lazy sibling who stood in one place too long). Mr. Williamson, you see, convinced his kids that the guy who thought up this holiday intended it as a day to see how hard you could work!

When Annie got to college and found out the rest of the world had been picnicking and watching parades while she was sweating over a paint bucket—well, Mr. Williamson's daughter sat him down for a word or two!

Annie's dad may have been conveniently confused about his holidays, but one thing he was right about: Kids need to learn the value of work and rewards.

We heard recently that McDonald's Restaurants and other fast-food chains were crying for workers. Kids no longer wanted jobs there because it paid only minimum wage, and pushing hamburgers seemed too strenuous in exchange for such a paltry sum. Some McDonald's franchises had to transport willing teens from miles away to take the jobs.

Stories like this make us nervous because we fear this "I'm-too-good-to-get-my-hands-dirty" attitude could fester in our kids, as well. Both Annie and I grew up in families of modest means. We learned to work hard because we had to, just to make ends meet. Above our fireplace, in fact, Annie has hung a painting of a tired Appalachian woman, hair pulled back in a severe bun, dressed in faded cotton and milking a cow. The picture represents her grandmother, she says, and her mother, and Annie herself as a girl. These people knew what it meant to labor diligently day after day with no choice of quitting, because their livelihood was at stake. Annie doesn't resent this representation of honest labor; on the contrary, she treasures the values her picture represents.

But I think about Heidi. When we glimpse the image of her childhood she may choose to hang above her fireplace, it won't be of a provident woman milking a cow on a frosty November morning. It may be a picture of her and her mother singing to an audience of a thousand, or trudging through an airport loaded down with baggage.

For the post-war generation, prosperity has meant we could give our children privileges we didn't have growing up. And for the most part, our children don't have to work to be sure there's bread on the table for the family. We're immensely grateful for the material blessings God has showered upon us, but in the midst of it all we want our children to learn the value of work and the value of money.

A thought that strikes me deeply is this: Many times a relay race is lost in passing the baton. I don't want to fail to pass the baton of hard work and money-sense to my children simply because our life circumstances aren't forcing me to do so.

Our children may well see a day when money doesn't come as easily as it does now. Their ability to sweat and scrimp may make the difference between surviving or sinking. And even if that doesn't happen, we believe knowing the joy of working hard and living simply will free them to live a happier and more God-honoring life.

Here are some guidelines we're learning to live by:

One:
Kids need to be given
opportunities to work.

When we give one of our concerts, the kids are expected to help. They have to sing when their songs come up, and to respond with courtesy and grace to the people we meet. And for the last few years, Nathan has been our traveling sound man.

We view these responsibilities as their contribution to the family business, just as Annie's heifer-herding was her contribution to the family farm. We pay the kids for each day they work with us on the road. I hope they aren't getting the idea that money falls from the sky, but rather, the harder they work, the more they will earn.

It seemed good to me, at one point, to also

teach them alternative ways to make money. Since the traditional options of lawnmowing and baby-sitting don't always fit well in our lives, I suggested to Nathan that he try a T-shirt business. The timing was perfect. He'd been wanting a hot pink BMX bike, but his cash reserves amounted to only $40. He figured that by the time he earned what he needed by going on concert trips, he wouldn't need the bike because he'd be old enough to drive a car.

I suggested he take his $40 and buy T-shirts to sell at the concerts. My son may not get A's on his math quizzes, but when it comes to his own money his brain becomes a high-speed calculator. "Dad," he argued, "buying $40 worth of T-shirts and reselling them will earn me a little, but it won't be nearly enough to get that bike." And what if the T-shirts didn't sell? He realized that by taking a risk he could lose what he already had.

He debated, and I coaxed. Finally, he decided to give it a try. In two concerts, he sold all the T-shirts. Say! This wasn't so bad! He took his profits and went back for more shirts, then more. In three weeks of selling, he turned his $40 into $400.

By this time I had visions of him owning AT&T by the time he was twenty-five! "Why don't you keep this up, Son," I prodded. "You could turn that $400 into a thousand!"

But the lure of that hot pink BMX called more loudly than my entrepreneurial urgings, and the entire $400 went for the bike. This bike, by the way, was *never* left out in the rain, or dumped in the driveway, or "forgotten" at a friend's house— because Nathan had toiled for it himself.

Later Nathan asked me, "Is it always that easy to earn money?"

"Not always. But if your product is a good one, and the price is right, your chances of treasuring a good profit are greater," I told him.

But he'd have to learn this maxim for himself. He tried marketing another time, but on that venture he lost money because the products weren't as desirable to the buyers. To me, this lesson was as valuable as the T-shirt success. Better to learn the principles of selling when $40 is at stake, than when the money needed to care for a family of your own is in the balance.

Not *all* the work kids do should earn them money, of course. Kids need to do some work simply to learn responsibility, and the life skills that will make them happy, productive adults. Nobody's happy living in a pig pen, though I'll confess Annie and I differ on just how clean the pen has to be to make it suitable for human habitation. She thinks a clean bedroom means all the clothes are hung in the closet. I call it clean if the clothes are dropped in piles orderly enough to find your blue socks the next time you need them without rummaging through the whole floor. You'll have to decide for yourself what example of "clean" you teach your kids.

One mom we know holds her eleven-year-old son responsible for the weekly vacuuming, cleaning a bathroom, and washing the dishes before he leaves for school (this in addition to making the bed and straightening his own room each day). And if she has to leave early for work, he's also responsible to see that the dog goes outside and the house is locked.

Her nine-year-old daughter regularly dusts, cleans a bathroom, feeds the dog, and is beginning to wash dishes.

"We started when they were toddlers," she explains, "by having them help pick up their toys. As they got old enough to make a bed, they helped me do it at first. When I knew they could do it alone, they did. And I had to ignore the urge to come behind them and remake it when it looked lumpy. When they did an especially good job, we made sure they got plenty of praise.

"Now, at eleven years old, Jason has to redo the bathroom if he doesn't clean it well enough. But when he first started the job, we only required that he do it. We would have broken his spirit by loading on too much at once."

This wise mom doesn't require her children to do *all* the household jobs on a regular basis, but she does make an effort to expose her kids to the skills they'll need as adults. "They've learned how to set the table, fold laundry, prepare a meal, wash the car, change a lightbulb—whatever it is they will need to do alone someday."

And she's convinced we have to start early. "If you wait until you think they're old enough, they're usually not interested anymore. Plus, they're so busy with soccer practice or piano recitals they barely have time." (And just about the time they're able to do the chores well, the brakes may go on in their willingness to help.)

Not every family will handle chores in the same way, of course, but I'm challenged by this family's commitment to prepare their two for the day when Mom won't be there to wash their underwear and Dad won't be around to grill the burgers. And at the same time, they're giving their kids a work ethic that will prepare them for the marketplace. If you had a restaurant, for instance, wouldn't you want to hire kids who already knew how to set a table or clean a floor? I would.

Two:
Kids need to learn to manage money.

Getting money is one thing. Figuring out what to do with it after you've got it is quite another. As the thousands of debt counselors across the country will tell you, doing the wise thing doesn't always come naturally. It has to be taught.

One of our recent lessons in this regard concerned buying on credit. Nathan and Heidi were already picking up from TV that "for just a few dollars down, and a few dollars a month, this super-juiced-up whatever can be yours." We tried to explain that those few dollars a month didn't really make it yours until it was paid for, but we could see we weren't getting through. So we went into the credit business.

The kids and I decided to buy a boat. All three of us wanted it, so I told them we could get it if they'd pay half. Both knew right away they didn't have the cash to pay half. That's when Steve Chapman's E-Z Credit opened for business.

"That's fine, kids," I told them. "I'll borrow the money from a bank. Each month when I pay you, you can give some of the money back to me to help make the monthly installments."

This sounded painless enough. For not much more than a little promise they were able to enjoy our new boat that very week.

The boom didn't lower until their next payday. To make the lesson as dramatic as I could, I made sure I had their wages in small-denomination bills, so they both looked like J. Paul Getty heirs as they stood there clutching their little wad of greenbacks.

"Now," I said, "first, you need to put away ten percent of your money for the Lord's work." This they did without question. (This habit has been a tradition at our house since the kids began getting money of their own. We're firm believers that God's admonitions and promises to givers apply to children as well as adults. And we believe that if kids don't learn the habit of giving when they're young, it will be a lot harder for them to do so as adults.)

They separated out ten percent and started to leave. "Whoa," I said. "Remember the boat? You promised to do your share to pay back the bank." Right. Both of them divided their stack of bills in half, handing one of the piles to me. What started out as an impressive wad had slimmed considerably. And what was worse, the same thing happened their next payday. And the next. And the next. And the next. This paying-for-the-boat idea was rapidly losing its luster.

We stuck to our agreement until their debt was cleared. And I doubt Donald Trump is any prouder of his yacht—if he still owns one—than my kids are of that secondhand boat. But two more important lessons came from it. One: Until it's paid for it isn't really yours—nor does it feel like it's yours. Two: Owing money is not fun. We've found those TV barkers with their "few-dollars-down" offers don't impress Heidi and Nathan like they used to. They learned the hard way that "buy now, pay later" really means "you'll keep on paying till you wish you'd never bought the dumb thing."

We're trying, too, to teach them some of the mechanics of money management. A couple of years ago I came across a pad of blank checks from an old account and decided they might be useful in teaching Heidi and Nathan about the wonders of the banking system. So we set up our own bank, and since with my gray hair I looked the most extinguished in the family I became the banker.

When the kids got paid, I'd give them a credit voucher instead of the cash and they could record it in their checkbooks. When they wanted to take in a movie or needed cash to head for the mall, they'd have to write a check and bring it to the bank for cashing. I'd trade their check for green money, and they'd have to do the appropriate arithmetic in their checkbooks. Both kids came away with a sense of what checking accounts are about.

And I discovered an interesting bonus. When my depositors came to make a withdrawal I'd ask, "What do you need it for?" Depending on their answer, I'd decide then whether or not to give them the money. (Think how much better we'd all do with our spending if bankers actually worked this way!) Heidi and Nathan are really going to be surprised when they take a check to a real bank and find you can withdraw all the cash you have in your account, and nobody asks you anything!

I've heard about one family who teaches money management in this way: In order to receive his weekly allowance, each kid has to produce a written record of what he did with his money from the week before. Those kids know to the penny where their money goes.

Teaching money management skills takes ingenuity and grit, but woe to the kids who face the wide world without them!

Three:
Most of all, kids need to learn the truth about what money can and can't do.

"Money can't buy me love"—and there's a host of other things it can't buy either. It can't buy satisfaction, or integrity, or success in God's eyes, or anything that really matters.

But Nathan and Heidi are growing up in a generation that proclaims, "The one who dies with the most toys wins." Because of this, Annie loves to remind us, "We shouldn't spend money we don't have, on things we don't need, to impress people we don't even like." Hearing it that bluntly stops me cold with how ridiculous this whole race to have more really is. That's why we're determined to find ways to live more simply and give more sacrificially—for our own good, and the good of our children.

I believe the best way we can fight greed is to give our money away. I don't mean all of it, of course, but enough to reach the level where it really costs us something to give. When we do this, the absence of money makes it harder to get the stuff we could do without.

We're giving our kids true riches when we teach the truth about work and money, because the best things in life aren't *things*!

5

Friendship

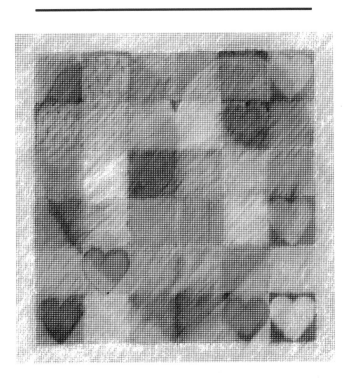

ANNIE: Steve's mother always seemed to have a flair for hitting children right between the eyes (gently) with the truths of Scripture. Her "rotten apples" lesson was no exception.

One year when the crop had just been harvested, she showed Steve and his sister a beautiful basket of apples she'd gathered. She'd made sure there wasn't a blemish in the lot.

Then, as the children looked on, she took a rotten apple and placed it in the middle of the basket.

Several days later, she gathered the children, and pulled out the basket again. By now, all the apples were rotten and stinking. Being mixed up with one bad apple spoiled a whole lot of good ones.

Talk about the time being "ripe" to discuss with her kids their choice of friends! To this day, Steve can't read the admonitions of Psalm 1, which talks about associations with the ungodly, without smelling rotting apples in the air. As the psalmist says, "Blessed is the man who does not walk in the counsel of the wicked or stand in the way of sinners or sit in the seat of mockers" (Psalm 1:1).

My mother was just as graphic as Steve's on the

issue of friends. "Annie," she'd tell me, "if you lay down with dogs you'll get up with fleas!" So when I read Psalm 1, I get a definite urge to scratch!

Both our mothers understood the power of friendship. A good one can make us; a bad one can break us. We want to help our children know why and how to choose for the good.

We need to protect our kids from harmful friends.

A couple of years ago Steve wrote a song called "Play, Little Boy," about a young boy whose mother took him along to a friend's house. While the two women visited, their young sons went off alone to play. But when the boys tired of the toys, one dragged out his father's magazines, thus exposing his friend for the first time to the seductive evils of pornography.

The innocent little boy in the song, it so happens, was Steve.

When he got home from the friend's house that day, he wanted to tell his mother what had happened. But he felt dirty and ashamed, so he kept the secret to himself.

The lesson to us from this experience is to not assume anything about the children who play with our children. Just because they live in the same neighborhood, or enjoy the same recreations, or even go to the same church doesn't guarantee they'll be uplifting friends for our kids.

One mom, whom I'll call Eva, tells of overhearing a neighbor child tell her five-year-old daughter, "Let's not tell your mom what we're doing with the Barbies." Of course this mother headed straight for the playroom to see exactly what the girls were up to. It turned out the neighbor girl had diverted from the typical "Ken-and-Barbie-have-a-wedding" games. Ken had become a sadistic rapist, who had stripped Barbie's clothes and was beating her with a whip. This shocked mother quelled her urge to deliver the century's sharpest lecture, and instead sat the girls down for a talk.

As Eva listened, she got the picture: This five-year-old's father consumed a steady diet of X-rated movies on cable TV, and when the child couldn't sleep she'd slip into the living room to watch with him. Her play simply duplicated what was acceptable fare in her home. The game was stopped, naturally, with a kindergarten-level explanation of "why we don't do things like that in our family."

From then on, Eva no longer allowed her daughter to stay overnight at this little friend's house. She did not end the contact, but wisely decided to monitor the influences her child was being exposed to by having the girls play at her house. From then on, she made her child's friends part of their family life. She also took the role of assistant Brownie leader, or Bible school teacher, or book report monitor at school, or swim team timer so she could know her child's friends and see them in a variety of contexts.

A watchful parent will casually move in and out of play areas to serve as a loving monitor knowing that it's not always the other family's child who can be a bad influence! Sometimes our little angel can be the rotten apple in the barrel, too.

As our children grow, our role of saying "yes" or "no" to friends becomes less, and we become more the coach and mentor in the child's process of choosing friends.

Heidi's friend, whom I'll call Betsy, is an example. Heidi became infatuated with Betsy in the way only grade-school girls can, but we were far from infatuated. Several traits in Betsy's character concerned us, and since Heidi at that time tended to be more a follower than a leader, we were concerned for Heidi's sake as well.

Betsy seemed quick to manipulate others for her own ends. Heidi wanted to invite her roller-skating one evening, so she asked Betsy if she could skate. Betsy assured her she could, so off we went. As it turned out, Betsy couldn't skate and expected Heidi to pull her around the rink all evening.

On other occasions, Heidi would come crying to me that Betsy had said mean things to her. Then Heidi's grades began to slide. It seemed Betsy didn't think getting your schoolwork done was "cool."

I was tempted to order Heidi to never see Betsy again, ridding her of this negative force that seemed to dominate her. But by doing that, I really would have been trading Betsy's domination for my own. Heidi would have learned little about discernment in friendships.

So we talked. When Betsy made Heidi cry, I'd ask, "Is this the way a true friend acts?" Or, "If you spoke to her like that, would you be behaving as a true friend to her?" Heidi always agreed this wasn't kind behavior, but her bond to Betsy didn't seem to weaken.

Sometimes I'd try to push her to confront Betsy. "When she takes advantage of you like that, just tell her off!" (Note the deeply Christian advice I gave my daughter . . .)

But Heidi would say, "I'm just not that kind of person, Mom. I don't want to hurt her feelings." And on it went. All I could do was pray, and invite Betsy onto our turf when possible in an effort to influence her in positive ways.

Not much seemed to change. To be honest, it was hard for me to act like an adult with Betsy. I would get angry because of the things she said to Heidi and I wanted to act unkindly to her. I realized that *I* had a choice to make. I could justify my anger to God—after all, my child was being hurt and shouldn't I lash out to protect her? I knew that I was beginning to use Heidi as my emotional whip. Because I was an adult *and* a Christian I couldn't emotionally lash Betsy myself. But Heidi could . . .

No! I could not teach my daughter in one breath about love and forgiveness, then turn around and teach her how to *blast* Betsy out of the water. *I* had to choose. I had to pray for grace to choose against these reactions.

It wasn't until the end of the school year that Heidi decided this wasn't a productive relationship. And on her own initiative, she broke off her "best-friend" status with Betsy. But Steve and I trust that year of difficulty helped Heidi learn to be more discerning in her choice of friends.

Make room for your kids to connect to positive friends.

One year at school, Nathan was invited to join a club some boys formed, in which the initiation rites included reading three articles in *Playboy* magazine! When he refused, a group of boys he'd hung around with all year decided they wanted no part of him.

Nathan came home in tears. "Mom," he said, "I feel like no kid in the world believes like I believe." But as I consoled him we remembered his friend Steven in Seattle, Washington.

It wasn't by accident the boys spent the following weekend together. Steven's commitment to the Lord is as deep as Nathan's, and they talked together about the sting of being booted from the "Playboy Club." But Steven was able to encourage Nathan in a way we never could, simply because he was his friend and peer.

Their weekend together reminded us that we needed to do whatever it took—buy the ball game tickets, give the extra time, host the parties, organize the overnights—whatever it takes to make space for the kids to be with positive, spiritually nourishing friends.

God revealed something very basic about our nature when He looked at Adam and said, "It is not good for man to be alone." The hunger for closeness is powerful, and when it isn't fed positively, negative friendships can take hold and fill the gap.

We must pray regularly that God will provide positive friendships for our children. We are not always wise enough to discern the real character of our children's friends. Some will remember the character, Eddie Haskell, on the "Leave It to Beaver" television series. When Eddie spoke to Mrs. Cleaver, he was the epitome of decorum. But close the bedroom door and he transformed into a terror!

Unfortunately, the Eddie Haskells are still with us. What seems to be a safe, wonderful friend may not be so at all. We need to bathe our children in prayer, asking God to reveal himself to them, to catch them in wickedness, discipline them when we don't know to, and keep them from evil.

Help your kids to make friends with their brothers and sisters.

Steve loves to tell the story of the little girl who knelt down by her bed to say her prayers. She'd barely started off with "Dear Lord," when her younger brother walked by and spotted those two little bare feet.

He reached down to tickle them, but his sister tried to ignore him as she went on with her prayer.

In another moment, the tickler was back. This

time she kicked out at him, but never broke the stride of her prayer.

A third time her brother tickled her feet, and this time she stopped. "Excuse me, God," she said, then turned around and knocked her brother into next Tuesday!

Needless to say, he never tickled her feet again.

My kids vacillate between sweetly praying for each other and wanting to serve up knuckle sandwiches. Today, with their bickering it's been knuckle sandwich time. And it makes me crazy. An equally exasperated friend called earlier and asked, "Did you ever want to sell your children?"

"The next caravan of slave-traders that comes through here and they're gone!" I said emphatically.

Nothing wears on me like Nathan and Heidi at each other's throats. Maybe it's because I love them both so much, and I can't bear to have *anyone* treat them the way they sometimes treat each other. Yet I'm faced with the sad reality that the perpetrator of the meanness to my baby is . . . my other baby!

At their best, however, they're wonderful. For Heidi's ninth birthday, Nathan wrote her a poem that he and Steve made into a song. It says:

> Here's to my sister—
> Remember every day,
> No matter what I've said,
> Here's what I *want* to say:
> I will always love you,
> Be with you to the end.

When no one else is around
I will be your friend.
I love my sister
And I always will.
I'm proud to be your brother,
That's how I feel.
And someday when you're far away
And the miles keep us apart,
I'm gonna whisper,
I love my sister,
And pray you'll hear it in your heart.[1]

Could these poetic sentiments have come from the same boy who just yesterday told his sister to get out of his room or he'd set her hair on fire? My dearest wish is that these two would become good friends. But friendship is a gift they have to choose to give each other. It can't be forced on them by me.

So Steve and I don't tell the kids they *have* to be friends. They don't even have to *like* each other. Two things we do insist on, though: They can't hurt each other, and they can't say mean things to each other. Even though emotions can't be legislated, respectful behavior *can* be. As long as the four of us live together, we will insist that our kids treat each other with respect.

In the worst times, I try to instill in them a vision for a brighter future. "There were times when I hated my brothers, too," I tell them, "but now I love them." Or, "When you two are grown, I know you'll enjoy visiting each other the way Daddy and his sister do."

---

[1] Times and Seasons Music. Used by permission.

Now, if you'll excuse me, I think I smell smoke coming from Nathan's room . . .

We need to model godly friendships for our children.

Who are *your* friends? How do you choose them, and what do you do to cultivate your relationship with them?

One friend I still hold dear is Lee. We met when Nathan was small and Steve was traveling with a band. Lee needed a sitter for her little boy, so I took the job. In our daily mothering exchanges our friendship began to grow.

Lee was delightful, so much fun to be with. And as she began to open up, I found she'd had a terrible life—two marriages, and a father who'd abandoned her—so I shared what I could of God's love for her.

One day she called, her voice full of excitement. "Annie, I've told you what a horrible man my husband is, so I'm going to leave my babies with him and go off to live with a 60-year-old man I'm in love with. I'm calling because you're my friend, and I want you to be happy for me."

My heart sank. Lee had gotten one thing right. I liked her very much and would have done almost anything to keep from offending her. But at that moment, I knew I had a choice to make, and I took a deep breath before I responded.

"I *am* your friend, Lee. And because I am, I can't be happy with your decision because I believe it's wrong." I went on to point out that she was wounding her children in the very way her father had wounded her. "The cycle can stop here, Lee," I pleaded. "Please don't hurt your children this way."

She didn't want to hear what I had to say. We never talked again, although I tried several times to get in touch with her. It's been years since then, and sometimes I still mourn the loss of our friendship.

Bad company corrupts good character. I didn't take a stand against Lee's lifestyle because I'm so strong, but because I'm weak. I don't trust myself, especially when someone's opinions mean as much to me as Lee's did. So when her priorities and values became opposite of those God had for me, I had no choice but to tell her she was wrong. And although I believe I did the right thing, it grieves me still.

And it's because of my weaknesses and my *desire* to become stronger in faith and deed that I choose friends who are stronger than I. I need to be encouraged, exhorted, and, yes, sometimes rebuked. My friends are people I can look *up* to, not perfect people by any means, but men and women who are "going on with the Lord," as the old expression goes.

In the final analysis, the basis on which we choose our friends can speak more loudly to our children than a hundred lectures on how they should choose theirs. That's why, little by little, as their understanding grows, I am sharing with my kids the choices I've had to make concerning friendships—and the consequences, such as what happened with Lee.

Steve sings about the paralyzed man in Mark 2, the one whose friends tore a hole in the roof so they could let him down to Jesus on a stretcher. When Jesus saw the faith of these friends, He healed the man.

Whenever I hear this song, I think: Who are my stretcher-bearers? What friends in my life help me get closer to Jesus? Which friends feel so committed to me they'd show this same kind of determination to help me in a time of need?

What our kids see in our lives—the friends we choose and the ones we choose to leave behind will teach them most of all.

6

Forgiveness

ANNIE: What would the world be like if Sigmund Freud hadn't come along and convinced us that everything wrong about ourselves is ultimately our parents' fault? Think of the television talk-shows, book publishers, and pop-psychologists that would be out of business.

Freud didn't really originate this "Blame Game," of course. It started back in the Garden of Eden. When God came to Adam and Eve asking, "Have you eaten from the tree?", Eve immediately responded, "The serpent deceived me, and I ate." (Twentieth-century translation: "The Devil made me do it.")

Adam was even more clever with his blame-shifting. "The woman you put here with me—she gave me some fruit from the tree, and I ate it." He pointed his finger at the woman, and at God for creating Eve in the first place, deciding that his own fall from grace was actually the heavenly Father's fault.

(Now I know where my kids get the capacity to come up with some of the clever blame-shifting stories they concoct. You've heard them, too. "If you hadn't bought me this tennis racket, it wouldn't have been right here when my sister made me so mad, and I wouldn't have been able to bean her with it, would I?")

Whether it's Freud's influence, or simply our sinful inclinations prodding us, we've become experts at pushing the blame onto our parents for every nasty weed we find growing in the garden of our life. The arresting thing is that our children will do the same unless we break the cycle of this destructive behavior by coming to terms with our own upbringing.

Of course sometimes blame rightly belongs on our parents' shoulders.

One day while Steve, Nathan and I were eating lunch, we started into recollections about the old days when Steve was still traveling with the group Dogwood. Nathan came up with a memory that surprised us. And it stung.

He could recall Steve coming home after several days absence, and then taking off again that same afternoon for another round of concerts. Nathan was three at the time and not able to express what he felt when Steve walked out that door, so we never guessed his dad's leaving impacted him at all. This happened only one time, yet in Nathan's memory it was magnified many times.

On that day at the age of twelve, when he recalled it, he told us how deserted and lonely he felt as the door closed and Steve was gone again. As he spoke, we could see by the sadness in his eyes and the slump of his shoulders, that the pain of that moment nine years before hadn't completely left him. All the trips to Disney World, picnics in the park, and family bike rides didn't erase his feelings of abandonment. My heart sank as I realized how wounded Nathan had felt by this incident.

A time of talking and praying and hugging followed the revelation.

Many of us came out of childhood bearing wounds inflicted by our parents' failures. For some, those wounds are so deep they seem as if they'll never stop bleeding. Maybe you were the baby unwanted by your mother, or the little girl molested by an uncle, or the boy abandoned by a father who walked out the door and never came back. Maybe twenty years of painful memories haunt you.

How can you expect to be a giving and forgiving person when you're trying to pour from an empty cup? It's impossible. But I believe there are three provisions God has given to help us fill those empty cups. When we take those provisions for ourselves we can then prepare our children to deal with the times ahead when their cups feel empty because of our failures.

God gives us the gift of forgiving.

I know of a grandfather, a mean-spirited and abusive man who treated his children cruelly. Yet his son Gary grew up to be one of the kindest, gentlest fathers.

I always took Gary's sweet nature for granted, until I began to realize what a statistical rarity he was. Studies show that child abusers invariably come from homes where they were abused as children. And the children they mistreat grow up to be abusive parents as well. The evil cycle goes on and on.

It made me wonder what happened with Gary. Why was he able to break the cycle of destruction? I believe I found the answer the day I went with him to the cemetery where his father was buried. He led me through the markers to his father's grave, and as I watched, Gary got down on his knees and began to dig up the soil around the headstone. Then he carefully planted a bright collection of potted flowers he'd brought with him. As he worked tears coursed down his cheeks.

The irony of it struck me. He was expressing grief for the memory of a man who had cruelly mistreated him. He had every reason to be planting thistles on that grave instead of flowers. But I knew from his actions that Gary had forgiven his father, and thereby transformed his innermost feelings toward him. By obeying God's mandate to forgive, God was able to heal the wounds in Gary and give him a tender sensitivity and love toward his own children's frailties and failings that overflowed to everyone.

Parents—it is high time we say it—are people too. I doubt that any parent looks down into his newborn's crib and says, "I'm going to shortchange this kid. I'm going to do all I can to be sure he grows up to be a desperate, grasping, needy wreck." Rather than deliberate acts of belligerence, the wounds our parents inflicted on us were more likely generated by ignorance, or reactions to their own childhood wounds that they didn't understand. And because every parent is an imperfect human being, our parents deserve our forgiveness. Healthy families happen on purpose: Unhealthy families happen by mistake.

When Jesus dined in a Pharisee's house, a sinful woman slipped in and washed his feet with her tears. In her defense, Jesus told the Pharisees watching, "Her many sins have been forgiven—for she loved much. But he who has been forgiven little loves little" (Luke 7:47).

I am saying this: God can use any parental failure for good. Our immensely creative God can see a way to generate right from the most abysmal wrong done to us—even the wrongs of our parents.

Now, what if parents' mistakes have been far worse than anything I've talked about thus far? I'm speaking of genuinely evil parents, whose cruelty still affects the child's adult life. If this type of situation describes you, it's even *more* vital that you work at forgiving your parents. Remember, God doesn't ask you to forgive them because they deserve it. But forgiving is the only way you can be set free from their influence and begin a whole new life.

Jesus explained it like this: "If you forgive men when they sin against you, your heavenly Father will also forgive you." But He goes on: "But if you do not forgive men their sins, your Father will not forgive your sins" (Matthew 6:14, 15). And the New Testament also teaches, "Judgment without mercy will be shown to anyone who has not been merciful" (James 2:13).

When we choose to be merciful to those who've hurt us, God in turn pours out His mercy upon us, so that the deeper the wounds inflicted, the greater the grace, love and mercy the Lord pours on those wounds in healing and comfort. For our God and Father is indeed "the God of all comfort, who comforts us in all our troubles, so that we can comfort [others] . . . with the comfort we ourselves have received" (2 Corinthians 1:3, 4). When we choose mercy and forgiveness, it is then we become partakers of the "good news" of God's grace. By choosing mercy, we open a locked door within, allowing His light and love to pour through, changing us as it touches others.

Make no mistake: Forgiveness is costly. It will cost you your "right to be angry." The reward, however, is glorious freedom.

The most graphic picture of costly forgiveness lavished on the undeserving is that of Jesus hanging in agony on the cross to gain heaven for those who nailed Him there. His words "Father, forgive them . . ." ring through the ages.

Christ's words can be your own—even if you have been severely, even repeatedly wronged. It *is* possible to forgive, no matter how painful or prolonged the offense.

After a concert, I spoke with a fourteen-year-old girl whose life had been completely broken by the sins of others. She never knew her father, because her mother was a prostitute. Lisa was molested by her mother's boyfriends, beaten by a malicious stepfather, and then taken from her home by Social Services, separating her from her six younger brothers and sisters whom she'd literally raised. Then during years of being shuffled from one foster home to another, she was sexually abused by a foster father.

As she told me her story, she sobbed, "These people knew what they were doing to me. How can I ever forgive them?"

As she spoke, I prayed about how to answer her. Again Jesus' words from the cross came to me: "Father, forgive them." It occurred to me in that moment that Jesus didn't say, "*I* forgive you." He asked His *Father* to forgive them on His behalf. When we do the same, our frail humanity meets God's limitless power of love, and the miracle of forgiveness happens.

Looking into Lisa's pretty, wounded eyes, I knew that many evils done to us have to be handled in this way. The sin is so great, the hurt so deep, we don't have the resource in ourselves to forgive. We must turn to God, the Source of all grace, and ask Him to do the forgiving, to act on our behalf. Nothing less could heal the wounds as painful as those suffered by the lovely young lady who stood before me.

I then encouraged Lisa to begin to pray for the people who had hurt her, that they might come to repentance and faith in Christ. The Sermon on the Mount tells us to pray for those who despitefully use us. Of course this is not easy to do, but it is the way to release and freedom, so that we can get on with a productive life. Lisa and I did pray together that evening—and the miracle of forgiveness began to work in her that night. I pray it continues.

A friend, Sally, showed the kind of grace I've been describing as she cared for her father during his last months, as he lay dying of cancer. I still marvel as I think of this woman, gladly tending to every need of the father who had sexually molested her as a child. Because I knew Sally, I knew that for years she had continually opened the inner doors of hurt to let in God's grace. I was witnessing the good fruit of her inner reliance upon God: forgiveness demonstrated. Showing forgiveness set Sally free, for the one who blesses is the one in control of the relationship.

Forgiving your parents can be the gateway to freedom for you as well. And practicing forgiveness will demonstrate to your children its benefits, preparing them for the day when they may need to forgive you for your parenting mistakes!

Steve penned this poem in regard to forgiveness:

> I opened up the prison door
> Used forgiveness as the key
> And when I let the prisoner go
> I found that it was me.

God gives us the gift of releasing our expectations and dreams.

Sometimes we act as though the Constitution guaranteed us the right to perfect parentage. So when we discover our parents were flawed, we feel outrage. A gross injustice has been done! (My dad missed my appearance as a ripe tomato in our second-grade Health Day performance! Call in Social Services and get me an attorney!)

But wait! If only flawless people could have children, you and I would have to join the ranks of the childless, wouldn't we? No one does it perfectly.

The Apostle Paul exhorted us in this way: "When I was a child, I talked like a child, I thought like a child, I reasoned like a child. When I became a man, I put childish ways behind me" (1 Corinthians 13:11).

Putting away childishness means giving up the expectations that my parents *should* have loved me flawlessly. It may mean letting go of childhood dreams we've cherished. For me, Christmases growing up were never the wonderful "Lennon-Sisters-TV-Special" fantasy I wanted them to be. That's why I determined that when I had my own home, it would be different. I would take control: make warm sugar cookies, have all the gifts carefully and beautifully wrapped early and under the tree, and sing carols around the fireplace. It would be a fantasy come true.

So when Steve announced that we would enjoy a simple and severely unmaterialistic Christmas I fought him tooth and nail. This was more than two newlyweds trying to blend traditions. For me, it was a struggle to save a powerful dream.

God asked me to give Him my dream, and to submit to Steve's desires for a simple Christmas celebration. I feared, of course, that giving Him my dream meant giving it up completely, but that isn't what happened.

Eventually, God softened Steve's heart. The celebration we now enjoy is a mix of Steve's Christ-focused simplicity and some of my tinsel-and-cider romanticism. Had God not taken control of my dream, though, I'd have orchestrated our Christmas into a production that might rival Macy's parade! In retrospect, I see that our Christmas may have lost the spiritual richness I really longed for.

When I quit trying to manipulate the present to repair the past, God can come in. He can make my todays beautiful, re-creating losses of the past into something wonderful and new.

And as my children witness the fact that I am able to give my expectations over to God and never be disappointed—they will one day know how to react and what to do when things in *their lives* don't turn out as they expected.

God gives us the gift of being responsible.

No person on earth will ever be able to give us all we need or desire. But healing takes place when we accept whatever love our parents were able to give us, and call it *sufficient*. When we stop trying to draw love from a dry well, we are free to turn to our heavenly Father and receive His love.

He fills our cup as He helps us to let go of our thwarted dreams and expectations. He also teaches us to take on adult responsibility: Maybe I was a victim as a child, but with His help I don't have to be one any longer.

Getting free of the "victim mentality" works in many areas of life. I can attest to that! Anyone who has known me more than two days knows I've spent a lifetime feeling fat. For many years, I *was* fat, and I could spend the next dozen pages telling you about the factors from my younger years that brought on those extra pounds. But there came a day when I decided those factors no longer need control me. They may have *made* me fat, but they didn't have to *keep* me fat. I was no longer a victim! I could choose life and health. So I quit saying I *couldn't* lose weight and started admitting it was because I *wouldn't*. This was a small step, but it was a start! Nobody had me in a strait jacket, punching me full of IV tubes to force extra calories into me. Nor was anyone holding a loaded gun to my head saying, "You finish off this cheesecake, or you won't see your next birthday!" Finally I acknowledged that the choice was mine—I was choosing to stay chubby.

Next came a major revelation. If I was choosing to stay chubby, perhaps I could choose not to. And slowly, I began to make different food choices—like munching on an apple instead of deep-fried catfish. I began to lose weight. It's been the fight of my life (and always will be), but the fight couldn't begin until I took responsibility for my weight.

Now I'm wondering what other childhood wounds can be healed as I look to God to help me put away childish attitudes and actions.

When I take responsibility for myself, I'm demonstrating to my children how they can be responsible to change themselves as well, no matter what help others do or don't provide. I'm leading them away from a self-pitying, victimized mindset into courage and the strength to change.

We owe it to our children to come to peace with our own parentage. We need to forgive our own parents, if that has not been done, and release unfulfilled expectations to God. We need to take responsibility for ourselves. Otherwise, if we live with bitterness, hostility, and unforgiveness, our children will stumble into adulthood crippled by our attitudes and failure to deal with them in a responsible manner.

You can be a bridge of reconciliation between your parents, your past and yourselves and between yourselves and your own children. One hand reaches back to our parents with the gift of forgiveness, and the other hand reaches forward blessing our children with a spirit that's free and at peace. Of all the legacies and gifts we can pass on to our children, the gift of a forgiving spirit is surely one of the most valuable.

7

Sexuality

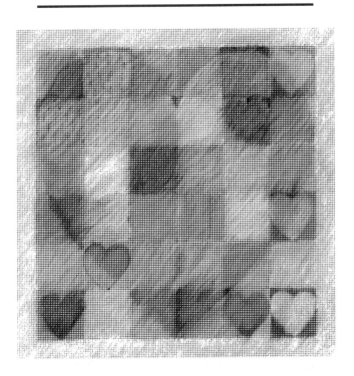

STEVE: Our parents laugh with us today at the minimal instruction we received from them about sex. For me, it was a hasty caution from my dad as I drove off to college—the proverbial, "Keep your zipper up, boy!" Annie's parents didn't go into much more detail. Her "birds 'n bees" talk with her mother consisted of another one-sentence warning: "If you get pregnant, it'll kill your father."

But Nathan and Heidi are growing up in a very different world from the one in which we did. Annie and I know they need a different kind of preparation in order to understand and enjoy their own sexuality.

We decided to set age ten as time for "The Talk." We would like to have waited until they were older, but were afraid we may be too late, considering the freedom with which sexual attitudes are broadcasted these days. We thought more specific information should come as late as possible, so the kids would be able to receive it with a degree of maturity. But impeding puberty pushed us to not wait until they were eighteen and ready to leave home. Before their bodies started changing, we wanted them to know what to expect and how to deal positively with those changes.

It wasn't as though sex was never mentioned in our home before the kids turned ten. But before then, we worked on communicating two basic messages that would prepare them for The Talk.

The first message: their bodies are wonderfully made, a gift from God. This one was easy. Daily life affords hundreds of opportunities to tell a little one, "Didn't Jesus give you nice strong legs?" Or, "Grandma says when you smile, your whole face lights up."

One mother we know tucked each of her preschoolers in at night with a song about all the ways God had made them special. Part of it went, "God gave you this nice body" (she'd pat a little shoulder or arm), "and your bright, healthy mind" (a pat on the head here). These children, through hearing and feeling, got a steady dose of reassurance that their bodies were good.

It was also fairly easy during the early years to talk casually about the obvious male and female differences, and to emphasize that both are good in accordance with God's plan. The kids, of course, noticed the plumbing differences between boys and girls early on. When they did, we took the opportunity to tell them that even though boys are born with certain more obvious equipment, girls have a special hidden place in their bodies where a baby can grow, so boys and girls are equally special and important.

Second, we indoctrinated them early with the fact that sex belongs in the context of marriage. It was not created for a man and a woman merely, but for a husband and wife. And some television shows which we've had to turn off have afforded us opportunity to point out that the endless scenes of undressing and lying down together shown on the screen are wrong because the couple are not husband and wife.

As an aside on this matter of TV, we may be more conservative than most about screening what our kids see. But it seems lately that you can't watch a cereal commercial without some couple hopping into bed. So unless the TV goes out the door—which wouldn't be a bad idea!—we've decided to monitor vigilantly and teach emphatically from what we see there.

So on the matter of sexuality, we decided that these two foundational ideas—their bodies are good, and sex belongs in marriage alone—were what our kids needed to know before The Talk. But if you have children, you've already guessed that Nathan and Heidi had their own ideas about what they needed to know most. Their friends, television, their own curiosity, and even songs from our own concerts (about temptation and the like) stirred up questions in their minds.

We took the position that all questions are good, and asking them was the right thing to do. But we tried to be wise in how we answered them. Kids sometimes ask, not because they're ready to hear the answers, but simply because they've heard the question. A simple answer is often all that is necessary to satisfy their curiosity at the time.

Child educator Maxine Hancock tells of a little girl who got a play-by-play description when she wanted to know how babies began. The little girl responded by wrinkling up her nose in disgust and wailing, "Oh, Mom! Did you and Daddy have to do that?" The child's reaction, Hancock said, isn't unusual when the facts presented are too explicit for the child's age and maturity. We agree with her when she concludes that questions should be answered clearly and crisply, but without too much detail. A simple answer like, "God has created a special way for babies to grow inside their mother's body" may be enough.

For some questions, we used the upcoming Talk as part of our answer. When Heidi came home once from a friend's house with questions, Annie told her, "Heidi, I want you to know all about the wonderful changes in your body that are coming. But I want you to get all the facts straight from someone who really knows. And I want to tell you when you're old enough to understand. If you'll wait until you're ten, there's not a thing you're wondering about now that I won't tell you then. You may hear a lot of things from your friends now that may or may not be true, but if you wait patiently, you'll get all the real scoop from me."

At that time, Nathan and I had already had The Talk, so Heidi knew waiting was an immensely attractive option. That's because in our family we made it into a grand occasion.

To make it a time he'd never forget, Nathan and I went to Atlanta to see the Hawks play the Chicago Bulls. We're talking about a night of watching Spud Webb, Dominick Wilkins and Michael Jordan crash around the court—boy heaven! I had arranged for Nathan and me to sing for the pre-game chapel service so that he got to meet many of the players. And—we went to the game in a Lincoln Continental I'd rented. After all, this was not a Chevy Citation weekend we were enjoying. We ate whatever food we enjoyed, stayed in a great motel and basically had a ball.

In the midst of it, I explained the mystery of sexual love between a husband and wife. And I did a fair share of warning about the obstacles ahead that would tend to deter him from enjoying his sexuality the way God intended.

I took Solomon as my model for these warnings. He wrote the book of Proverbs to teach his own son wisdom. To that end, he includes several passages that deal explicitly with sex—both how to enjoy it within marriage, and how to avoid misusing it outside of marriage. I wanted to give the same wisdom to my son.

Annie and I pulled most of the information we presented in The Talks from an excellent tape series and book by Dr. James Dobson: *Preparing for Adolescence.* Dr. Dobson's years of counseling teenagers helps him focus on what kids most need to know. And his warmth and wit make the information easy to receive. Some parents like me listen to the tape series with their children and then talk over their responses. I decided also to translate the material into the West Virginia dialect Nathan has come to expect of me. This approach seemed to work.

When we finished, I gave Nathan a glass filled to the rim with water, and asked him to carry it across the motel room. (I'm the one, remember, whose mother used rotten apples to warn me about friendships. So over the years Nathan has gotten used to my making strange requests, suspecting when a "lesson" is going to follow.)

Anyway, when he made it across the room, I asked, "Nathan, how did you manage to keep from spilling the water?"

"I had to be really careful, and pay attention," he replied.

"Son, that's just what I want you to do with all the things we've talked about this weekend," I said. "I've told you a lot, man-to-man. And you'll need to be careful how you use this information. You mustn't spill a drop of it to your friends."

It must have made an impression, because later when we were driving down the highway he blurted out, "Daddy, I want to pray!"

Normally I greet a request like this with enthusiasm. But at that moment, I had one hand on the steering wheel, and the other clutched a dripping Big Mac. In our family, prayer together usually includes taking hold of the other's hand. In light of the discussions we'd just had, I figured this would be one of those times when that extra reassurance was definitely in order. So with one hand I held the Big Mac, pressing my knee firmly on the steering wheel, and with the other I took Nathan's hand. (Please, do not try this yourself . . . I should have had more sense!)

"Lord," Nathan began, his voice choked with intensity, "I want these hormones to be *part* of my life, not *all* of my life. Please help me to stay sexually pure until I get married."

When he finished, he wasn't the only one with tears in his eyes.

The next day at church, Annie noticed Nathan looking surprisingly serious as he studied a group of junior-high kids sitting a few rows ahead of us. "What's wrong, honey?" she asked.

"I guess I'm just feeling a little sad," he said. "It'd be nice to be just a regular kid like all the other kids and not know about all this stuff."

One idea had come clear: Sex and responsibility are inseparable. We think that's a healthy mindset for a boy or girl entering the teen years. As they get older, Nathan and Heidi will understand sexuality in a broader light—as part of what bonds Annie and me so closely, and as the wonderful process that brought them into our lives. Now they see it more as a treasure to be protected, and that's great, too.

You may be wondering about Heidi's experience with The Talk. Well, as you may have imagined, the girls did *not* choose a basketball game. Instead, they dressed to the teeth, and with a cassette player and James Dobson's *Preparing for Adolescence* tapes in hand, plus enough luggage for a week, they set off for a weekend at the famous Opryland Hotel, a place so elegant (and so expensive) that Annie and I have never stayed there ourselves!

Nathan and I had flowers waiting for them in their room, along with a note reminding them of our love and prayers. To cap off the weekend Annie presented Heidi with a gold key to symbolize the key to her heart and purity. (I'd given Nathan a similar gift at the close of my weekend with him.)

It is our hope that each of our children will present the key to his or her spouse on their wedding night as they begin a new life together.

Needless to say, Annie reported that the weekend she and Heidi shared was as special as Nathan's and mine.

But there's more to teaching about sexuality than The Talk will cover. A significant amount of inappropriate sexual activity among kids has less to do with their hormones than with a basic, human need for affection.

Psychiatrist Marc Hollender interviewed 100 women who had had three or more unwanted pregnancies. The women differed in many ways, but in one way they were alike. Nearly all the women said they had never been meaningfully touched by their fathers. Many of them saw their sexual activity not as an end in itself but as a means to get the non-sexual touching they craved.

I believe much of the wholesome affection these women long for should have been supplied by their fathers as they grew up. That conviction is what prompted me to write a song called "Her Daddy's Love." It warns fathers that if they aren't willing to supply the appropriate affection daughters need, their little girls will more than likely seek that warmth inappropriately from other men.

The letters of response that song has evoked has only deepened my conviction. One woman wrote:

> My father took very little interest in my life as I was growing up. Because of the business my parents were in they had no time for me or for a normal family life. I suppose they did

the best they could, but I grew up feeling terribly insecure.

When I was about twelve years old, I began being noticed by boys. By my mid-teens I was involved with men much older than me. It seems I was always looking for men who looked like my dad.

I married young, after becoming physically involved with a young man. I felt so guilty and knew what I was doing was wrong. Two children later—we were divorced. I know now that I was just looking for my daddy's love.

The hunger for love that women like this one expressed motivated me to look for ways to show Heidi how special she is to me. That's why I sat up and took notice when I met Bill Hornsby from Louisiana who was adored by his four teenage daughters. (Yes, that's right—four teenage daughters! They're gone from home now and he survived, but he didn't see the inside of his bathroom for ten years!)

When I asked how he'd developed such a warm relationship with his girls, he shared his secret. He set up a "date night" once a week, during which he'd invite one of his girls out for dinner. That way, each of the girls had her own night out with Dad once a month.

This sounded like an idea I could manage, so I went right home and invited Heidi out for an evening with me. I'd even allow her to choose where we'd eat.

Since she was only two years old at the time, I wound up dressing up in my McSuit and McTie, and having a McWonderful dinner. (As she's gotten older, her taste in restaurants has improved—but so has the size of the check!)

I try to make these evenings as special as possible. Sometimes I bring her flowers, or buy her a little gift. And I make a special effort that our conversation doesn't turn into a lecture, or focus on problems. Normal life has enough of that. The date is just to let my daughter know how much I love her.

Besides taking her out, I consciously work at being affectionate toward Heidi as she moves into her teen years. Psychologists say it's common for fathers who regularly hugged and kissed their daughters while they were small to withdraw physically once their girls begin to mature. Maybe we feel uncomfortable with our little girls as they blossom toward womanhood, but if we withdraw it only makes them feel the changes they're experiencing must be bad.

Wanting to feel loved is a God-implanted desire, and He intended it to be met in the context of our families. If we fail to provide the affection that is needed, our kids will look for it elsewhere. And we all know there are too many out there with wrong motives who are ready to prey upon a young girl in search of affection. I can't afford to withhold healthy affection from my daughter, and neither can you.

I encourage you to take to heart the words of my song:

> Daddy, you're the man in your little girl's dreams.

You are the one she longs to please.
And there's a place in her heart that can only
   be filled
With her daddy's love.
But if you don't give her the love she desires,
She'll try someone else but they won't satisfy
   her.
And if your little girl grows up without daddy's
   love,
She may feel empty and it's only because . . .
It's her daddy's love that she's looking for.
Don't send her away to another man's door.
Nobody else can do what you do; she just
   needs her daddy's love.

Someday if you hear that her purity's gone,
She might have lost it trying to find what was
   missing at home.
Let the heavenly Father heal where you've
   failed.
He can forgive you and help you to give her
The daddy's love that she's looking for.
Don't send her away to another man's door.
Nobody else can do what you do; she just
   needs her daddy's love.[1]

It is equally important that I find ways to express my love to Nathan without embarrassing a
thirteen-year-old who's very conscious of being
"cool." But boys need their father's embrace as
much as girls do.

After we'd sung "Her Daddy's Love" at a concert, we received a wrenching letter from a man
who confessed to years of struggle against ho-

---

[1]"Her Daddy's Love," Dawn Treader Music. Used by permission.

mosexuality. "You could have called your song 'His Daddy's Love,' because the need is just as deep for boys," he wrote. Soon after, a friend who works with AIDS patients told us that 95 percent of homosexual men lacked a loving relationship with their fathers when they were young.

To encourage dads with sons, I was inspired to pen these lyrics:

> There are those who cannot understand
> Why a man would take a man for a lover.
> And if you would ask him he might tell you,
> I was this way when formed in my mother.
> But there are other words written in his life,
> Hidden in his heart, but seen in his eyes:
> His heart is cryin',
> "I need my father's embrace, I've tried other
>   men's arms
> But they cannot replace
> The touch I have never known.
> I needed it as a child, and now that I am grown
> I still need, I need my father's embrace."
>
> He was once that little boy who stood in line
> Behind the other things his daddy held so
>   dear.
> And he waited for his turn, but it never came.
> Now he's a man with a heart full of little boy's
>   tears—
> 'Cause through the years no one has told him
> There's a Father above, holding out His arms,
> Reaching down with love.
> He hears him cryin',
> "I need my father's embrace, I've tried other
>   men's arms
> But they cannot replace

The touch I have never known.
I needed it as a child, and now that I am grown
I still need, I need my father's embrace."[2]

It may sound as though I'm ignoring the importance of mothers showing affection to their children, but that is not my intention. Most moms I know do this a hundred times better than men do without even trying. We fathers seem to have to work at it harder. But when we do, the rewards go on for generations. That's enough to make me more conscientious about taking the time to express my love to my children.

In the final analysis, giving our kids plenty of affection seems to be the best preparation for encouraging a healthy acceptance of their own sexuality. We also allow our own children to see us kissing, hugging and holding hands. Although they need information, nothing gives them a sense of security like a healthy dose of expressed affection between their parents. And with the solid teaching that the sexual relationship is reserved for the golden container of marriage, our children will be equipped to know what to do and what not to do when it comes to making their own choices regarding behavior in a relationship.

To God, sex is not a bad word. He intends that we enjoy our sexuality. We can help our kids discover that the real joy of sex lies in following God's intended plan for it.

---

[2]"Father's Embrace," Times and Seasons Music. Used by permission.

8
Laughter

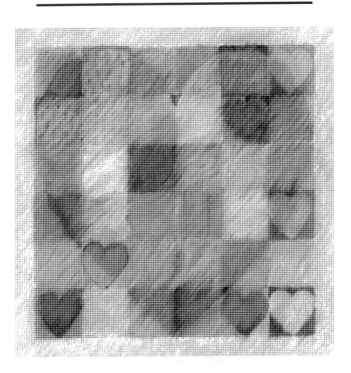

ANNIE: The year was 1980, I was nine-and-a-half months pregnant with our second child, and Steve was on the road. I was definitely not in a laughing mood. This time, his group was off doing concerts in the Pacific Northwest, as far away as it was possible to be from me and still be in the continental United States. I know this, because I measured it on the map, and rehearsed this information to myself every time a twinge of false labor made me gasp.

The pregnancy had been awful anyway, but toward the end I developed unexplained fainting spells. I'd be walking down the hall, and—*clunk*—I'd keel over. My doctor thought it had something to do with variances in my blood sugar level, so he recommended I carry a pocketful of Hershey's Kisses. When I felt the least bit faint, I was to pop one in my mouth. For a woman who for years thought chocolate was one of the four basic food groups, no doctor's prescription could have been more welcome, so I went right out and filled a grocery basket full of Hershey's Kisses.

All this chocolate did nothing to stop the fainting spells. But ever hopeful, I kept inhaling them anyway as I watched my thighs balloon.

Finally it all got to be too much, and I went wailing into my doctor's office with a tale of woe sad enough to inspire a week of episodes for *As the World Turns*. The baby was coming any minute . . . Steve was out of town . . . I was fainting all the time . . . I couldn't drive the car . . . and I felt so fat and awful!

My doctor looked at his sorry specimen of a patient and gave me these tender words of consolation: "Annie, lighten up! Your baby's going to be fine; you're going to be fine; Steve will make it home for the delivery. Don't take life so seriously!"

This tough response was not exactly what I expected, especially from a man who had just weeks before ordered me to subsist on Hershey's Kisses! Yet it was the right response. I did and I do take life far too seriously. It's unquestionably healthier for my children when I don't.

Not long ago, I heard about a father in Colorado Springs who asked his teenage daughters to evaluate their parents. The two girls took pencil to paper and came up with a varied list of what they didn't like. But on the plus side, both girls had one item written in big letters and underlined: "You make it fun to live here." And both agreed the one positive outweighed all the negatives.

When I heard that, it reminded me of a quote I'd read from psychologist Erich Fromm: "Today's children need happy mothers as desperately as they need loving mothers."

I thought too about a challenge from Barbara Cook, the author of *How to Raise Good Kids*:[1] "Lots

---

[1] Published by Bethany House Publishers, Minneapolis, Minnesota, 1978.

of loving mothers make miserable persons out of their offspring simply because they refuse to be happy people themselves."

She must have known my precious grandmother, whom I adored. Though she had a long list of fine qualities, my grandma had one little flaw: The day she was born, she started waiting for her death. I remember as a girl, walking those four miles up the hollow to see her. We'd sit on the porch and visit—she in her rocker and I on the step. And every time as I stood to leave I'd hear the same sad farewell: "Well, child," she'd drawl, "the next time you see me you'll be lookin' down at me in that ole' pine box." No amount of reassurance would shift her morbid focus.

Of course, the next time I'd walk up the hollow there she'd be—rocking away. And I'd say brightly, "Grandma, you said the next time I'd see you, you'd be dead. But here you are, fit as ever." She assured me that she may have eluded Fate this time, but wait until next time. And as I'd leave, she'd tell me again, "Honey, I expect you'll be seein' me in that ole' pine box . . ."

Just a couple of years ago, I called my mother with the unhappy news that we wouldn't be able to come home for Easter. She heaved a heavy sigh, and then said, "Well, if you can't come see me now, I guess the next time you see me I'll be all laid out in that ole' pine box . . ."

"Mother!" I broke in. "Don't start that! Grandma told me that for forty years before she up and died."

"See," my mother retorted, "she was right."

How do you argue with logic like that? Sometimes laughter is the only possible response. Tim Hansel rightly observes, "Humor has the unshakable ability to break life up into little pieces and make it liveable . . . Life really is fun, if we only give it a chance. Countless moments of serendipity are constantly alive to us and inviting us to participate, if we but have eyes to see, ears to hear, and hearts to respond."[2]

We owe it to our children to help them see the humor in life—for the sake of their sanity, their health, and their relationships with others.

Laughter keeps us sane.

There should be a law that says you can't have children unless you're able to laugh, because laughter can make the difference between survival and insanity! We should have known the minute they told us it started with something called "labor" that raising kids was not going to be a picnic.

Take the woman with three young children who looks at parenting and observes: "Children are demanding by nature. They make most of those demands on their mothers. 'Where's my schoolbag?' 'I need 67 cents today.' 'My jacket is ripped.' 'I'm out of clean underwear.' 'Why don't you make pies anymore?' 'Can I order these books from the book fair?' 'I need a physical exam for camp.' 'I need a sack lunch every third Thursday in months ending in R.' 'I'm bleeding!' 'Can

---

[2]*You Gotta Keep Dancin'*, (Elgin, Ill.: David C. Cook Publishers, 1985), pp. 82, 83.

I go to Kristin's house?' 'It's raining, can Scott and Mike and Jason and Eric play here?' 'I feel hot.' 'Read me this book—*All the Nursery Rhymes in the English Language*' 'Read it again!' 'Sew on my Girl Scout patches.' 'Fix the hair on Raggedy Ann.' 'Can we fingerpaint?' 'Can we make puppets?' "

After she and her husband had adopted their first three, this same woman began to feel unusually fatigued and sick each morning and—oh yes!—she was pregnant. After the baby came, she reported, "It was a hysterical pregnancy. I was pregnant, and my husband was hysterical."[3]

But learning to laugh is far more than just a way to keep parents sane. When we give our children the gift of humor, we are teaching them an absolutely vital element in getting through life's difficulties.

Viennese psychiatrist Dr. Victor Frankl was imprisoned in a Nazi death camp during World War II. Many things, including his passion to see his wife again, kept him alive. But he also knew the necessity of humor.

Early in his captivity, he and another prisoner promised each other to think each day of one funny story about what could happen to them after they were released. "Humor was another of the soul's weapons in the fight for self-preservation. It is well known that humor, more than anything else in the human make-up, can afford an aloofness and an ability to rise above any situa-

---

[3]Quoted in "Mommy Wants a Real Job," Sandye Tillrock Voight, *Redbook*, June 1987, pp. 6–7.

tion, even if only for a few seconds. . . ."[4]

Comedian Bill Cosby has said, "Once you find laughter, no matter how painful your situation might be, you can survive it."

Teaching our children the value of humor ranks right up there, in my book, with teaching responsibility and self-esteem and forgiveness, which are the other necessary elements in the art of sane living.

Laughter will make you healthier.

The Bible says, "A merry heart does good like medicine." That fact has been verified by the medical profession. Psychologist David Mc-Clelland found that after a group of medical students watched a funny movie, the infection-fighting proteins in their bodies increased.

William F. Fry, M.D. , of Stanford University, who has studied laughter for thirty years, calls it "inner jogging." He says a long, hearty laugh every day does your cardiovascular system as much good as ten minutes of rowing. Sounds good to me! I never understood those silly rowing machines at the gym anyway, and all that sweating makes my perm friz. Laughing is more fun, and it doesn't require $114 shoes and a shower afterwards!

Laughter seems to be God's provision for releasing the natural pain-killers in your body that combat arthritis and slow down the release of

---

[4]Dr. Victor Frankl, *Man's Search for Meaning* (New York: Pocket Books, 1969), pp. 68, 69.

stress-producing hormones. It may not be long before your doctor advises, "Forget the aspirin. Take two belly laughs and call me in the morning." Already nurses at Oregon Health Sciences University wear buttons proclaiming: "Warning: Humor may be hazardous to your illness."

Laughter helps keep life in perspective.

Heidi was sitting at the kitchen table, dawdling away on the assignment in her Bible notebook that was due the next day, when Steve and Nathan burst into the kitchen. "There's a great movie playing downtown," they announced, "and if we leave in fifteen minutes we can just make it."

"I look awful," I protested, "and fifteen minutes isn't enough time to get myself together."

"I'm not inviting you to a beauty contest," Steve shot back. "It's a movie, and it'll be dark there anyway. And what about that message we just heard about making wonderful memories for your children? Remember how they told us the most treasured ones would come from these *spontaneous adventures?*"

Guilt won me over and I agreed to go, but I insisted Heidi finish her schoolwork first. So there's Heidi, scribbling answers as fast as she can, while the rest of us hunch over her like pesky flies, buzzing, "Hurry up! We're going to miss the beginning. Can't you go any faster?"

When she scratched in the last answer on the page, Nathan grabbed her arm and bolted for the car. I stuffed the workbook in my purse, and Steve and I hurried out after them.

On the way to the movie, I opened Heidi's notebook to look over her answer and her assignment sheet fell out. Oh no! This wasn't the only page she had to complete. She was supposed to do the entire chapter.

"Stop the car," I groaned. "We've got to go back. Heidi's assignment isn't done." So we went back to the house. The men decided *they* didn't have an assignment due, so they'd take in the movie without us. As they drove away, Heidi started to cry.

Guilt got the better of them, though. Heidi and I weren't home alone five minutes before Steve and Nathan trudged in the door. Compared to the complaining that followed in that living room, the Israelites in the wilderness would have sounded like an Optimists' Convention. It went on until I absently muttered, "It's that silly Bible assignment! Having to look up all that Scripture ruined our great family time . . ."

When the absolute stupidity of what I was saying, and the craziness of what our family just experienced got through to me, I started laughing. I laughed till I cried. Laughing over how ridiculous we were acting put things back into focus and salvaged what would otherwise have been a very bleak evening.

Humor can do that. It can help us to see the big things as big as they are, and the small things as small as they are. (By the way, we all blamed Steve for suggesting such a harebrained idea, and decided to *plan* a family excursion for the next evening. Sometimes *spontaneous* isn't always the way to go.)

Laughter takes the hard edge off parental sternness.

Once we asked the kids to compile a list of the things we most often said to them. This is what they wrote:

- I'm not talking just to hear my jaws flap.
- You just ate.
- You'll make it till breakfast.
- It'll be good for you.
- Sit back and buckle up.
- Not another word.
- I had to walk five miles to school and five miles home and it was uphill both ways.
- Don't touch each other.
- There are starving people in Africa.
- When I was a kid I had to eat dirt for breakfast.
- Were you born in a barn?
- Don't you look at me like that.
- I'll give you something to cry about.
- Ask your mother.
- Ask your father.
- That drives me nuts.
- Do you want to live to see your next birthday?

- If you pick at it—it won't heal.

Then there are the mixed messages like:

- Shut your mouth and eat.
- Hurry up and don't run.
- Don't be smart.

Has formulating this list caused us to stop saying these things? Of course not. But at least laughing together about them makes it slightly less nausea-provoking to the kids when they're repeated for the eight-zillionth time.

There's no place in parenting for "jokes" that ridicule or put down children. But all kinds of room exists for humor that replaces sarcasm, or diffuses genuine fury. There are days with Heidi and Nathan when, listening to songs about how sweet children are (even ours!), I wish the tape would self-destruct. On one really rough day I told the kids, "Here's a parenting song I'd like to write: 'I've got bald spots on my head, from tearin' my hair out over yew-w-w-w-w.' "

Humor is the spoonful of sugar that makes the medicine of all our serious parenting efforts more palatable to children.

Keep up the laughter.

In a world where every hourly newscast burdens us with reports of rapes and murders and bombings, it's not easy to find the lighter side of life. We have a few ideas that may help.

Be with people who help you laugh. Solomon

wisely said, "There is a time for everything . . . a time to weep and a time to laugh" (Ecclesiastes 3:1, 4). Our closest friends know how to weep. They've cried with us over personal losses, and decried together the terrible things going on in our society, like the tragedy of abortion. But they also know how to laugh.

They can find the humor in the most mundane of life's moments, and when we're with them we find as much to laugh about as to cry about.

Collect laugh-starters. Steve and I have gotten hooked on the homespun stories of humorist Garrison Keillor, because every time we hear them they tickle us again. Some people we know save jokes and cartoons that get them giggling. If a video makes you laugh, buy your own copy. It's cheaper than a psychiatrist!

Look for ways to laugh when you don't feel like it. Psychologist William James said, "We don't laugh because we're happy—we're happy because we laugh." I detect some Christian truth in that thought. In a parallel, I don't always feel like reading the Bible, but when I do, the "want-to" usually follows.

It's the same with laughter. Life with Christ *is* full of joy, but I don't always feel that joy. Sometimes working to find the humor in my day uncorks the joy of the Lord that was in me all along.

Our kids also keep us laughing, if we let them. I remember one day that seemed far too long. I'd done the work of three women, I thought, and wanted nothing more than to fall into bed. So I was less than sympathetic when Heidi began to beg for a bedtime story. I hollered from the bathroom, "Okay, just one story and that's it." And I plodded down the hall to her room.

"Mom, you promised just one story, is that right?" Heidi asked too sweetly.

"That's right. Only one," I said firmly, as I sat down on her bed.

"Okay," she grinned menacingly, "I want to hear the story of the *Thirty-Five* Little Pigs!"

Ha-Ha—right?

9

Good Choices

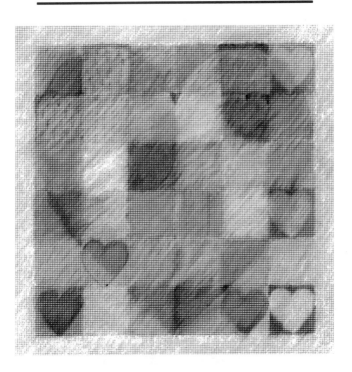

STEVE: The belief in "original sin" has always been rather unsettling to me. Like many parents in my generation, I would rather assume a child's naughtiness was motivated by ignorance more than anything else. If only parents would instruct their little ones in how to behave, the sweet cherubs would jump at the chance to do right.

That was until Heidi came along. Never was there a baby who looked more angelic than Heidi, with her luminous blue eyes, and round little face, circled with wispy brown curls. But when she turned two, all our illusions of her angelic perfection crumbled.

When she decided to have her way, she didn't rant and shout, or scream "No!" as many kids do. Instead, she'd simply withdraw, and do it so completely she almost seemed in a trance. For instance, when I'd pray at the dinner table, we'd each finish the prayer by saying "amen" in turn. But when this rebellion began, at Heidi's turn she'd respond with a blank stare. A time or two we let it pass, but then we realized a pattern was developing. We had to act.

Six months of steady confrontation followed.

Sometimes we felt like candidates for The Meanest Parent Award as we insisted Heidi obey. For instance, when she refused to sit down, we'd make her sit. She'd kick and scream, but as Annie restrained her she'd say quietly but firmly, "Heidi, you will not win. You must obey." Finally, Heidi would yield, and a time of sweetness would follow. But we lived in dread of the next episode.

One of these came during a visit to the pediatrician's office. The doctor wanted to weigh Heidi and she said brightly, "Heidi, you're a big girl now. You don't have to sit on the scale. I want you to stand."

As the doctor attempted to help her stand, Heidi's eyes narrowed and she drew her feet up beneath her. Annie knew what was ahead, and left the room.

Twenty-five minutes later, the doctor emerged with Heidi in tow. The doctor's hair had been neatly braided. No longer. Her hair hung in tangled disarray. Both she and Heidi were drenched with sweat.

"I hope you understand, Mrs. Chapman," the doctor said. "I had to win—for Heidi's sake."

"I know, Doctor," I responded, "and you have merely tasted her wrath. I live with it!"

Seeing the doctor's determination gave us courage, and we needed it because these confrontations exhausted us. Heidi's resistance was so intense I wondered if we were battling the forces of evil on her behalf. But no matter the source of her rebellion, it had to be met and quelled, or we knew she'd never be free to choose to do what was right.

Children can't make good choices if their "choosing mechanism" is weak.

As we tackled Heidi's strong will, we took courage from a true story about three-year-old Sandy and her mother, Mrs. Nichols, related by Dr. James Dobson in his book *Dare to Discipline.*

Dr. Dobson says, "On the afternoon prior to our conversation, an incident occurred which was typical of Sandy's way of doing business: The mother put the youngster down for a nap . . . Sandy began to scream. She yelled loudly enough to upset the whole neighborhood, fraying Mrs. Nichols' jangled nerves. Then she tearfully demanded various things, including a glass of water.

"At first Mrs. Nichols refused to comply with the orders, but she surrendered when Sandy's screaming again reached a peak of intensity. As the glass of water was delivered, the little tigress pushed it aside, refusing to drink because her mother had not brought it soon enough. Mrs. Nichols stood offering the water for a few minutes, then said she would take it back to the kitchen if Sandy did not drink it by the time she counted to five. Sandy set her jaw and waited through the count. '. . . three, four, five!' As Mrs. Nichols grasped the glass and walked toward the kitchen, the child again screamed for water.

"Mrs. Nichols and her little daughter are among the many casualties of an unworkable, illogical philosophy of child management which has dominated the literature on this subject during the past twenty years. This mother had read that a child will eventually respond to patience and tolerance, ruling out the need for discipline.

"She had been told to encourage the child's rebellion because it offered a valuable release of hostility. She attempted to implement the recommendation of the experts who suggest that she verbalize the child's feelings in a moment of conflict: 'You want the water, but you're angry because I brought it too late'; 'You don't want me to take the water back to the kitchen'; 'You don't like me because I make you take naps'; 'You wish you could flush Mommy down the toilet.'

"Unfortunately, Mrs. Nichols and her advisors are wrong! She and her child were involved in no simple difference of opinion: she was being challenged, mocked and defied by her daughter. No heart-to-heart talk would resolve this nose-to-nose confrontation, because the real issue was totally unrelated to the water or the nap or other aspects of the particular circumstances . . . Sandy was brazenly rejecting the authority of her mother. The way Mrs. Nichols handled this confrontation would determine the nature of their future relationship."[1]

I believe that when a child surrenders his will to his parents—which in God's authority structure means giving his will to God—the will then becomes truly strong so he is free to use it to choose righteousness. All this "Just Say No" stuff we're teaching our children is fine, but we're expecting children with wills as weak as spaghetti to be able to use them like iron rods to beat off

---

[1]Dr. James Dobson, *Dare to Discipline* (Wheaton, Ill.: Tyndale House Publishers, 1970), pp. 1, 2. Used by permission.

evil. Our help is coming twelve or fifteen years too late. At two, they should be learning, "I will say 'yes' to Mommy, even though I don't want to." Then at fifteen, it's more likely they'll be strong enough to say, "I can refuse drugs, even though I don't like losing some friends."

We need to let our kids practice choosing whenever we can.

One day at the barber shop, Nathan decided he was bored with the same old haircut. He told Annie, "Mom, all the kids have this totally *rad* hairstyle—" (you know—that's short for "radical," meaning a "good" thing) "with *lines*."

I discovered he meant straight lines, shaved down to the bare scalp. Annie thought the whole idea sounded ugly at best, masochistic at worst. And what would people at our concerts think when we showed up with a teenage boy whose hair made him look like an escapee from a concentration camp?

But Annie told herself that Nathan *is* a young man, not a baby, and that in the blink of an eye he's going to be out from under our roof, making all the decisions of his life alone. This hairstyle choice wasn't going to affect his health, or safety, only our pride. And it might prove to be an excellent and low-risk practice ground for independence. So she told him of her reluctance, then gulped and said . . . yes.

The results were as awful as she feared, but she said nothing. Fortunately, Nathan didn't like the haircut any more than Annie did. He hadn't envisioned anything quite *that* "rad."

In this situation, hair—or the lack of it—wasn't a moral issue. So it presented an opportunity to practice gathering information (from friends, from Mom, from his own wishes), then making a decision.

As the children grow older, we're continually on the alert for times like this when they can learn decision-making skills, because they've got a lifetime of decisions ahead of them.

Children need to see that their choices have consequences.

I grew up with a clear understanding that stealing was wrong. But when, at age six, I saw a red toy car at Queener's Hardware, all that good teaching turned mute. I stuck the car in my pocket and walked home.

When my mother saw me playing with the car, she realized at once it was new. She also knew I had no cash, so it didn't take long to extract a confession from me.

To think her child had shoplifted must have embarrassed her immensely, since my dad preached regularly at a local church. But instead of trying to cover over the theft with a "boys will be boys" excuse, she marched me straight down to see Mr. Queener, to return the car and to apologize for what I'd done. I was scared silly. Would this mean a jail sentence for me? Obviously not, but this lesson was to prove immensely important years later when I had a son of my own.

When Nathan was much younger, we were driving across west Texas when we spotted a roadside fruit market and decided to stop. It didn't take us long to make a purchase, and we headed on toward our next concert stop. Thirty minutes down the road, Nathan got our attention. It seemed that while he was wandering around the market, he'd picked up an orange.

I knew what must be done. I turned the van around, and back we drove to the fruit market where my son had to stammer out an apology for the wrong he'd done in taking what didn't belong to him.

To be honest, we were tempted to ignore the crime and eat the evidence, especially when confession cost us over an hour of driving time. We knew the fruit merchant would never miss one orange, and it was no major blow to her business.

But we knew also that if Nathan stole an orange and suffered no negative consequence, he'd be learning from experience that crime does pay: What an easy way to get things you want without having to part with a cent!

This fruit-lifting incident ended with a surprise twist for all of us. After Nathan talked with the market manager, he climbed back into the van feeling awful. Though we'd talked often about the fact that we all sin, Nathan had never felt the burden of guilt before. So in these moments, when he clearly felt he needed forgiveness, was the perfect time to explain how Christ can take away our sins. When Nathan heard the gospel clearly presented at the point of his need, he was ready to repent and accept Christ's cleansing. In that van, somewhere in west Texas, he asked Christ to come into his heart.

How glad we were we hadn't chosen to take the easy way out! Letting him experience the consequence of his choice to steal opened the door for him to see his need of grace.

On the flip side, our children's positive choices have positive consequences. And they need to know it. When their attentiveness in school earns their teachers' praise, we need to pass those praises on to them. When they work hard in our concerts, they deserve the applause they receive at the end. Every child who does well at his home chores, sports, schoolwork or whatever, deserves to have that good work acknowledged. Proverbs 3:27 tell us, "Do not withhold good from those who deserve it, when it is in your power to act."

After our kids make choices, we need to help them stick to them.

I heard not long ago of a father in New York who gave his daughter great freedom to choose the high school sports she wanted to participate in. He enthusiastically paid for whatever equipment and uniforms she needed and faithfully cheered her on at games and meets.

His only requirement was this: when his daughter chose to begin a sport, she had to finish the season. The track season tested his requirement to the limit. Though practices seemed like fun at first, the newness soon wore off, and sleeping late sounded more inviting than rolling out at 6:00 A.M. to run. Then his daughter pulled a ligament. The two friends who'd joined the team with her dropped out. Her boyfriend began to nag her about how much time track practice demanded. She had plenty of reasons to quit.

But her dad stood firm: even if she finished unhappily, she'd finish. A commitment made needs to be kept, whether or not it is easy.

She did finish the season, though not without some unhappy complaints. But in the end, she beamed with pride that she'd stuck it out when her friends had quit.

It's impossible for me to think of living out a tough commitment without Annie's parents coming to mind. Her father had a heart attack at age 51. While his life hung in the balance, we watched her mother "sleep" sitting up in a straight-backed chair night after night because she refused to leave his side. Now, after 47 years together, Annie's mother is battling cancer, and it's her father's turn to give when the giving costs him immeasurably. Just because the going has gotten tough, neither of them considers getting out.

Our children will never learn this kind of commitment if we don't help them stick to their choices when things don't work out as they've planned. Psychologist Kevin Lehman explains it very practically. It's great to say, "Tommy, would you like a tuna sandwich or peanut butter and jelly?"

But what happens if he says he wants tuna, and after Mom has it ready, he switches gears and decides on peanut butter? In the interest of keeping peace, we're tempted to stick the tuna in the fridge, and whip up a new sandwich.

But Dr. Lehman warns that this response teaches my child that commitments mean nothing. It doesn't matter if he chooses tuna, because he doesn't have to stick to his choice if he changes his mind later.

If he says he wants tuna and then decides he doesn't, let him go hungry until dinner, Dr. Lehman advises. He'll think more carefully the next time you ask him to make a choice because he'll know he needs to stick by his choice.

Is one little sandwich really worth this hassle? We believe it is. It is one small but strong step in building stick-to-it-iveness. On a greater scale, Jesus admonishes us, "No one who puts his hand to the plow and looks back is fit for service in the kingdom of God" (Luke 9:62). He wants us to keep the commitments we make to Him. But children don't magically become faithful in their commitments when they turn 21. They learn to be faithful by living out the consequences of their small choices, and thereby grow in their capacity to follow through on major life decisions.

We hope our doggedness on those peanut butter/tuna selections will eventually help our kids to think more carefully before they make a purchase or choose a career or even select a mate, because they know they have to follow through on those choices.

Children need to be taught discernment, not just do's and don'ts.

Music is one issue in our house on which we don't set a lot of hard and fast rules. Although we have told our kids, "Heavy metal rock music is not permissible," more importantly, we work hard at equipping Nathan and Heidi with the tools they need to discern good from evil.

For instance, we pay attention to the words of popular music and talk with our kids about them. And we look at album covers together. So many rock groups use satanic signs or symbols of bondage or just plain grossness on their covers, that it's not hard for the kids to discern that this type of music tends toward darkness and away from God. This takes some effort on our part to stay up with the world of music, but we feel it's worth it.

Not long ago, I took Nathan to hear a Christian recording artist. On the way home, I asked, "Nathan, what did you think about that singer?"

"She was pretty," Nathan responded, and then went on to give a future sound man's evaluation of the relative mix of vocals and instrumentals. Then he asked for my reaction.

I had come away from the concert with some cautions. Though the music was entertaining, its message wasn't clear. And the singer's revealing mini-skirt didn't seem to be in keeping with her Christian identity, to my way of thinking. So I carefully shared these observations. Nathan was quiet for some time, then said, "I see what you mean, Dad."

"I didn't want to cut her down," I told Annie later, when we were alone, "because some kids will be helped by her concert. But I liked the chance the concert gave for Nathan and me to talk over some of these things."

Talking about why we respond as we do builds a foundation. It's like Jesus explaining the Kingdom mindset in the Sermon on the Mount, rather than simply handing down the Ten Commandments. He was teaching us the *basis* for making choices, instead of drawing hard lines.

We can follow His example with our kids, as well. And we can believe the Holy Spirit will help them draw the right lines when their day comes to make choices on their own.

10

Vision

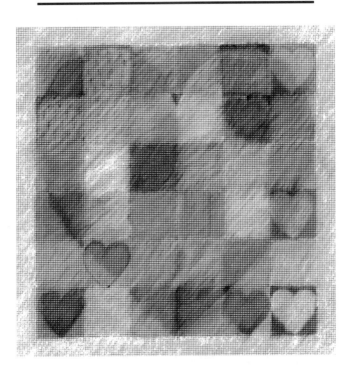

ANNIE: The Chapman family spends so much time traveling, sometimes I feel like airports have become my "neighborhood."

So, in the interest of keeping my neighborhood from being taken over by evil, I've on several occasions confronted airport newsstand operators about the pornographic magazines they sell. I tell them these offend me and why, and then ask them to please consider removing them.

I've received mixed responses. Some say, "I'm glad you said that. I feel terrible selling these magazines. I'll pass your complaint on to the manager." Others say, "Look, Lady, I only work here. It's a free country, ya know."

But there was one reaction I never expected.

At one stop-over we were waiting in the boarding area for our plane. The call to board came a bit earlier than we anticipated, so as we gathered up our bags, Steve whistled for Nathan, who was heading off toward a gift shop. Thinking he was after gum or a snack, Steve waved wildly to motion him back. But Nathan had other intentions.

He turned toward Steve, and with one hand made a motion as if he were unsheathing an imaginary sword. Then he turned and headed into the gift shop.

We knew then what he was up to—this determined eleven-year-old was off to wage war against pornography. He'd stood by while we spoke out, and he'd decided he wanted to make a stand as well.

A few moments later, he emerged from the gift shop with a grin and slid that imaginary sword back into its sheath.

Steve and I were delighted. We dream that our children will want to change the world they live in. We hope they'll grow up to be more than nice people, with clean fingernails and well-groomed lawns and paid-up taxes, who don't do anybody any harm. May they want to give themselves to something larger than their own comfort!

That's why we involve our kids in the struggle against evil. Like the time we joined a protest against abortion at a local Planned Parenthood clinic. It did not turn out to be a Sunday school picnic. A firefighter from the fire station across the street from the clinic became more and more angry as he watched us. He finally came after me, verbally assaulting me and threatening me physically. I was determined not to be scared off from this battle to save innocent babies, so I stood my ground as he became more and more irate. Finally, he left. I tried to hide my terror so as not to give him the satisfaction of seeing how shaken I was. (Steve called the fire chief when we got home, and received an apology and assurance that behavior like this wouldn't happen again.)

Should my children have been present to witness this ugly encounter? Definitely! And they were. They need to learn that fighting in God's army isn't just a colorful metaphor their Sunday school teacher thought up. We are soldiers, and fighting calls for courage in the face of danger, tenacity in the face of resistance.

None of our family went to jail that day, but some of our friends have, and the children know it. Now when they sing "Onward, Christian soldiers, marching as to war . . ." it's with a different sobriety.

I wish it didn't have to be this way. I wish we could shelter our children from the fact that our government sanctions the deaths of some 4,000 infants every day. The weight of information like this steals away the simplicity of their childhood, and that's sad. But we're living in a war zone, and you can't shelter warriors.

Other children are warriors in different ways. I love the story counselor Gary Smalley tells of the time his college-age son was being belittled for being a virgin. The young man turned to his peers and said, "Look, I can join your club any time I want to, but you can never join mine!" What a great response!

Other teens lead Bible study and prayer groups in their schools. Or "do battle" more quietly as they invite friends to church, or come to the defense of the "class nerd," or choose to tell the truth when lying would be much easier.

May they fight! But let's help them fight in ways best suited to the temperaments the Lord has given them. Nathan loves a head-on confrontation. The challenge of it gets his adrenalin pumpin' and his eyes a-blazin'. (A bit of his feuding West Virginia mountain heritage showing through here, I think.) Though he struggles with the same fears of being ridiculed that we all do, confronting someone isn't as costly for him as it is for Heidi.

Heidi harbors a gentle heart. She's the one, remember, who didn't face her friend's manipulations for a year because she couldn't bear to hurt the girl's feelings. That's why it didn't surprise us when she said she'd written a letter to the President, asking him to stop abortion. Confronting by means of a protest letter is less threatening for her. But we reassured her it's just as important as any other method, because it's Heidi's attempt at joining the battle. She doesn't need to fight in the same way Nathan does in order to be a soldier in God's service.

There was the time in an airport, however, when Heidi came hurrying down the concourse to find Steve and me, her face flushed. She was trembling. Immediately, we wondered if someone had tried to hurt her.

"I'm all right," she said, her voice shaking. "But I just told that lady in the book place I didn't think they should be selling those dirty magazines in there."

We never would have suggested Heidi go alone to do something like this and she knew it. And she may never feel the calling to do it again. But at that moment, it seemed to her to be a question of standing up for the right, or running away. How proud the Lord must be that she chose to stand, even though she was scared silly. (We were proud of her, too!)

Helping our children to become warriors develops in them a desire to *save* the darkening world. But a second kind of desire matters just as much. They also need the desire to *heal* a broken world. We want them to appreciate the beauty of a life poured out in service to the lost and broken people around them.

One Thanksgiving, early in our marriage, Steve and I took our meager funds and bought the ingredients for a family-sized feast. Then, as the turkey roasted in the oven, Steve took the car and went out to invite street people to share the meal with us. Our inspiration for this rather unusual Thanksgiving celebration was taken from Matthew 22:9: "Go therefore to the main highways, and as many as you find there, invite to the wedding feast," (NASB).

Our limited financial resources (that's the year that we grossed just $3000 dollars) had allowed us to purchase only a modest-sized turkey. Nonetheless, Steve came driving up with a stuffed car full of hungry and eager dinner guests.

The Thanksgiving prayer not only included the praises of a thankful heart, but also a request for God to multiply the food to feed these hungry "multitudes." As it turned out, there was plenty of food. More importantly, we had a chance to share the love of Jesus and the message of hope with some folks who needed the help and comfort of a loving Lord.

Other families have sacrificed their privacy and comfort to take in foster children, to provide a haven for an unwed mother, to care for a handicapped baby, or to look after a Southeast Asian family as they resettle.

One family we know took their children to Haiti to help build a mission church. The country they chose is one of the most destitute in the world, so there were none of the "creature comforts" these middle-class, Nintendo-addicted children were accustomed to. The kids spent stifling nights tossing and turning under mosquito nets (no air-conditioning here!). During the day they moved rocks, shoveled dirt—and developed blisters, right alongside the Haitians they'd come to serve.

I couldn't help but wonder if this brave mother ever worried about what she'd feed the kids if the local food didn't agree with their little stomachs. "I took along a huge jar of peanut butter," she told me. "I figured if worse came to worse, they could live on peanut butter sandwiches for two weeks . . . they do at home!"

As it turned out, the children survived just fine. They came back to the U.S. with a vision to help, rather than always receive.

Sometimes it takes determination on our part to help our children give. I recall the time Nathan heard a plea on The 700 Club TV program for money to fight the evils of our society.

Nathan wanted to help, and decided to give $20 a month for the next six months. Though I was pleased with his zeal, I knew $20 would totally drain his cash resources, so I suggested he pledge

$10, and he bounced off to phone in his pledge.

Not long afterward, Nathan received a reminder envelope with a notation about his $10 gift. Now that the time had come to part with his money, the passion that motivated his promise had faded. The reminder letter collected dust on his desk.

Occasionally we reminded him to "send in the money," but other more enticing uses for his cash kept popping up. Another month came, and another reminder. Nathan still did not respond.

Finally Steve confronted him. By not keeping his promise, he'd lied to The 700 Club. So Nathan tightened his belt, did extra chores, pitched in some gift money and ultimately kept his pledge. He parted with the $60 with a mix of reluctance and pride.

Did we discourage our son from helping others by insisting he follow through? We don't think so. Our children must learn to keep commitments—and that anything worth fighting for is going to require something of them. If they grow up expecting the battles to be too easily won, or won only by others, reality's harsh blows will cripple them and keep them from giving consistent, productive service to others.

When Jesus healed the woman with the issue of blood, the Scripture records, "At once [He] realized that power had gone out from him" (Mark 5:30). We should expect it to cost us, as well, when we give ourselves for the healing of others.

One thing needs to be made clear, though. When we serve, there are no guarantees that the wounds of others will completely heal, or that the world's evils will all disappear. A nine-year-old's letter to the President, or an eleven-year-old's home-made placard held high at a demonstration probably won't turn our nation around. Even for me, there are many days when I feel my small attempts to stand against evil, or to help those in need are about as effective as trying to sweep back the ocean with a whisk broom.

But we can't do what's right because we're guaranteed we'll make a difference. We do what's right because it's right to do what's right. God calls us to faithfulness, not necessarily to success. If history turns, so much the better. We want to be faithful to Him whether it turns or not.

I often tell Heidi and Nathan the story of the starfish. You may know it. One morning an ocean-side village awoke to find their beach covered with starfish. The tide had swept them in, and then left them behind when it receded. As the day warmed, the starfish would all surely die. But since the job of saving them looked so immense, no one tried to help.

Late in the morning, a man walked onto the beach, only to find a small boy picking up one starfish after another and throwing them back into the ocean.

"Little boy," the man said, his voice tinged with disdain, "there are thousands of starfish here. What you are doing won't make a difference."

The boy simply picked up another starfish and threw it back into the ocean. "It makes a difference to this one," he said.

Our feeble protests to a few newsstand operators may not bring the *Playboy* Empire to its knees.

But maybe one porn seller will begin to think . . . then two.

Even if we don't see evils like abortion and pornography abolished in our lifetime, or all the world's wounds healed, our children will be better people for having been in the fight. When we give them the marvelous gift of godly vision, we open in them the capacity to live for something greater than themselves.

In his novel, *The Laird's Inheritance*, George MacDonald says it this way:

> The inheritance of your earthly father may be this land about us here, an inheritance that is dwindling, and which we may lose some day. But the inheritance of your Father in heaven, a father who owns the cattle on a thousand hills, and all the hills of the earth, is an inheritance no one can take from you. And that is the legacy I want to leave you, my son, a heritage of righteousness, of truth, of love for God, and of service to your kind. This is a more lasting inheritance than any earthly fortune that I could pass on to you.[1]

We want to teach our children that they are not only the leaders of tomorrow, they are an important part of today. They will either be a part of the problem or a part of the solution. We want to train them as worthy warriors to have vision for the solution. If our children see in their parents a willingness to work, to part with financial

---

[1]George MacDonald, *The Laird's Inheritance* (Minneapolis: Bethany House Publishers, 1987), p. 33.

resources, to give time, and to live for the cause of Christ and decency, then they will have a clearer vision of the challenge that lies before them.

11

Spiritual Legacy

STEVE: Nothing we teach our children matters more than teaching them to love God. Any other gift we might give them—a good self-concept, solid business experience, positive attitudes, social skills, sexual common sense—any of these mean little if they aren't connected to the Lord of Life.

It sobers me to read the scriptural accounts of godly men whose children did not follow the Lord. God called David "a man after my own heart, who will fulfill all my will." Yet his son Solomon gave in to the lure of idol-worshiping women and bloated materialism. Another son killed his brother, another raped his half-sister, a forth tried to overthrow his father's kingdom.

Eli was another man of God, a priest chosen by the Lord to mentor the prophet Samuel. But Eli's own sons blasphemed God, and Scripture says, "He failed to restrain them." God punished both Eli and his sons with death.

You would think Samuel would have learned from this dramatic end to Eli's family, but when he had sons of his own he failed with them, as well: "But [Samuel's] sons did not walk in his ways. They turned aside after dishonest gain and accepted

155

bribes and perverted justice" (1 Samuel 8:3).

When I read the books of the Kings, it seems as though the tendency to godliness (like the tendency to deliver twins) can skip a generation. One king would serve God: his son would be a rascal; his grandson would return to the Lord. And on it went.

A friend of ours who is a pastor's wife wonders if this observable trend could point to what she calls the "theory of reaction." You know: If your parents are neat-freaks, you'll be sloppy; you keep your home spotless, but your kids think an order to "take out the garbage" means you want them to date people of low repute!

When it comes to passing on a spiritual passion, I don't believe it has to be this way. Listen to what God says: "My Spirit, who is on you, and my words that I have put in your mouth will not depart from your mouth, or from the mouths of your children, or from the mouths of their descendants from this time on and forever" (Isaiah 59:21).

I'm actively on the lookout for ways to fan the flame of love for God in Nathan and Heidi. The four ideas that follow may help.

We need to pray for them.

I start here because it's where my parents started with me. If you knew my mother, you'd know why I say that.

I cannot forget the time during my teen years when she came into my room, waking me out of a half-sleep. She dropped to her knees by my bed, and without a word to me put both her hands on my arm and began to pray, "Lord, you know what is ahead in Steve's life. If you see that he's not going to be faithful to you, then I pray that you'll take him home to heaven *right now!*"

This struck terror in my heart. But you need to understand Mom. She was a woman with a hotline to heaven. We often heard her pray specifically, and more than once the answer arrived almost before she said "amen."

So I lay on that bed shaking as I waited for a 10,000-volt blast of lightning to incinerate me.

Only because God is merciful am I still here. But you can see my mom took the notion of praying for her children very seriously.

Sometimes Mom's prayers seemed to connect her to God in a way I didn't like. During my years in the Navy I got away from the Lord and got messed up with drugs. My folks must have known I was up to no good, but when I came home on leave I went to extremes to hide these habits from them.

Once when I came home for the weekend, the house was empty and I found they'd gone to a church convention. It looked like the safest place I'd found yet to do drugs, so I stuck around. I smoked some pot, and then decided my pipe needed cleaning. The six pipe cleaners I used did the job, but they also left me with a dilemma. How was I going to get rid of them? If I threw them in the trash, my parents might find them and realize what I'd been up to.

I wadded the pipe cleaners up as tight as I could. Then I wrapped a napkin around them, grabbed the Campbell's soup can I'd just emptied, ripped off the lid and stuffed the napkin with the pipe cleaners into the can. Then I put the lid on top, and filled up the rest of the can with more napkins.

This is just the beginning! An empty milk carton was on the kitchen table, so I put the soup can into the milk carton, then packed it full of crumpled newspaper and closed the top as best I could. Then I took all the trash out of the wastebasket, placed the milk carton in the bottom, and covered it completely with trash. I was sure a kennel full of dogs, trained to sniff out sodden pipe cleaners, could never have found that stuff.

Drug dogs have nothing on the God who sees all.

Two weeks later I came home again. Sunday morning my mom stopped in my room to ask if I was going with them to church. I groaned and said I would, but in a tone of voice that said I'd sooner be covered with honey and staked to an anthill. She didn't lecture me, but just before she left my room, she turned around.

"Son," she said, "I have another question for you. Whose pipe cleaners were those in the trash?"

I nearly fell out of bed! Did this woman have X-ray vision? "How in the world did you know they were there?"

She answered, "I was praying for you, Steve, and the Lord impressed me to go look in the trash for pipe cleaners." She paused, and looked at me sadly. "I didn't think I'd ever find them!"

That memory isn't the happiest of my younger years. I couldn't fool God. And because of the way prayer connected my parents to Him, I couldn't fool them either. But my sin needed to be confronted, and having to face the reality that I was hurting those I loved was part of what drew me back to Christ. My mother's prayers helped me in ways her advice never could have. I trust my prayers will do the same for Heidi and Nathan.

We need to tell them what we believe.

When Jesus wanted to describe a near-impossible act, He said it was harder than trying to push a camel through the eye of a needle. I have another illustration. From my experience, it would be easier to squeeze a camel into the needle's eye than it is to get kids of any age to sit through family devotions. We've tried everything, from coaxing and cajoling, to threats that we know we could never carry out.

But as our kids get older, they're not the only ones resistant to family devotions. We adults fall prey to the "put-it-off syndrome." It's easy to let devotions slide.

At present we're working at reading through the New Testament together. And no matter how difficult it becomes to make time for this family Bible study we're determined not to surrender. We'll do whatever it takes to expose these kids to God's Word, because there's no way for them to know what we believe unless we tell them.

Just as important as the readings of Scripture, are the "readings" they get from me as I apply God's Word in daily life.

As I mentioned in an earlier chapter, I'm afraid to fly. Annie knows it. The kids know it. Yes, I know it's safer than driving a car, but when I hear those jet engines start to rev up, no logic in the world is strong enough to keep my stomach from jumping up into my throat. As you can imagine, my prayer life has improved considerably since we started flying to concerts.

Sometimes I feel these fears make me a poor example of a faith-filled daddy. But then it occurred to me that perhaps faith is going ahead and facing what you fear, trusting God will care for you whether you feel safe or not. So each time we land safely, the four of us catch each others' eye and mouth the word, "Ebenezer." It's a name I found in 1 Samuel which means "Thus far has the Lord helped us." I trust hearing these hundreds of Ebenezers from me will also help set Heidi and Nathan's hearts to expect the Lord's help when they're afraid.

It's fine for me to have faith, but unless Nathan and Heidi hear me talk about my faith journey, they won't know what I believe, or why I make the decisions I do. Our kids need to hear us read God's Word, but they also need to hear how we're thinking about ways to make those words real in our lives. The Christian life is a walk, as we're fond of saying, but it must be a talk, too.

We need to make truth something they can see and touch.

After the children of Israel entered the Promised Land, the Lord instructed them to take twelve stones from the Jordan River to build a memorial to God. God explained, "In the future, when your children ask you, 'What do these stones mean?' tell them . . ." (Joshua 4:6).

God certainly laid the groundwork for getting our kids' attention! Give them something to look at, or a mystery to solve, and they'll remember it far longer than the most eloquent lecture you can deliver.

My dad knew this instinctively, it seems.

One year at youth camp, he was to speak to the teens. Before the camp, he went down to our hometown's finest jewelry store. There he chose the biggest, gaudiest watch he could find. It must have cost him no more than $1.50, but it looked like it was worth a thousand bucks. Its luminous green face glowed and the rhinestones sprinkled all over it glittered.

That night he preached one of his most passionate sermons on why kids should keep their lives pure. He was tired, he said, of dramatic testimonies from converted alcoholics and members of motorcycle gangs who hit bottom before they decided to obey Christ. He said it didn't have to be that way for us.

Then he stopped, and appeared to totally change gears. "I want to give somebody a watch," he announced, holding up that glittering prize. "Who'd like to have it?"

Every hand in the place shot up.

He looked over the crowd, then chose a young man sitting near the back and asked him to come up and receive his prize. Elated, the boy rushed to the podium.

The boy had hold of the strap, when suddenly my dad pulled it back. Reaching under the podium, he pulled out first a brick, and then a hammer. He laid the watch on the brick, and before anyone understood what he was about to do, he smashed the watch with that hammer. Pieces flew everywhere as the startled crowd gasped.

Then Dad gathered up the pieces and placed them in the hand of the disappointed young man who stood before him. "Don't destroy your life like that before you give it to God, because if you do it'll break His heart."

I can't remember one other sermon from all my years at youth camp, but as you can see, that one stuck with me for more than 30 years. Visual images are powerful tools to communicate God's truth.

To make our children's experience of the Faith a more visual one, last year for Christmas we gave Nathan a beautiful old English-style sword. To us it symbolized the passing of God's Word, the Sword of the Spirit, from father to son. And we hope he'll one day pass both the sword and the Sword to his son or daughter.

Will one three-foot hunk of metal establish his bent toward godliness? Not in itself, but we hope it'll be one more link in a long chain of influences that will help him be true to God and His Word.

A friend named David challenged us with a fresh approach to giving children a tactile exposure to the doctrine of the Trinity. He told us this story:

> My boys and I were reading the Bible over breakfast one morning and Joel, my seven-year-old, said, "How can God be three different people? I thought you said there was only one God." "There is only one God," Aaron, my nine-year-old, said proudly. "God is God. Jesus and the Holy Spirit are not God." Then, looking at me with less assurance than he'd just voiced, he said, "Isn't that right, Dad?"
>
> I was frantically flipping through the Bible dictionary in my mind (small as it is!), trying to head off rampant heresy in my own kitchen. How was I going to explain something the church fathers could only handle in delicate theological phrases, like grains of rice between chopsticks, in the early Creeds? How was I going to explain what it meant to be "one in substance with the Father . . ."?
>
> *Substance.* It occurred to me in a flash. I knew of only one readily available substance that exists in three distinct forms and yet is the same substance.
>
> Going to the freezer, I picked one ice cube out of the bin. I passed it from one child to the other, explaining how water freezes, and in the form of ice is useful for certain important purposes—like keeping our food from rotting, and cooling drinks.
>
> Then I put the ice on a plate, and stuck it

in the microwave. As it rapidly melted, I reminded them about how water is good for
drinking, and keeping living things alive.

Then I poured the newly formed puddle
off the plate into a small pan, and set it on a
burner atop the stove. In a couple of minutes
it was in the form of steam. To illustrate the
properties of water as it reaches the steaming
stage, I poured it into a clear glass, then
dropped in a tea bag. In a moment the boys
could smell the herbal aroma.

My teaching points went like this: God the
Father is the one who saves the world and
keeps us from spiritual death by His unchang-
ing Word, just as ice preserves food. For some
men, God's Word seems hard and cold because
they don't like it. For others, it's the best thing
there is because it saves their life.

The Son is like water, I explained, washing
us clean of sins, giving us joy, and making our
soul feel as good as if we'd just taken a long
cold drink on a hot summer day.

The Holy Spirit brings out the fragrance of
Jesus Christ. He moves about as invisibly as
water when it turns to steam. He lets the
power of God and the good character of Jesus
come through us the way steaming water releases the flavor in a tea bag.

I know that picky theological-types might
take exception to this homey lesson, but nine
months later my seven- and nine-year-old
boys still talk about the different aspects of
God. Believe me, it helped me to understand
a question I'd wondered about many times as
an adult.

In Jesus, the Word was made flesh and dwelt

among us. Jesus was touchable truth. And since He's no longer physically with us, we want to find other ways to make his truth real to our children. They hear it plenty. They need to handle and taste it also.

We need to help them
see God at work in them.

We'd been having problems with a bearing in one of the wheels in our trailer. I decided it probably needed repacking and I set to work taking apart the wheel. Heidi, then six, sat down on the tire I had just removed to watch me as I removed piece after piece of the wheel mechanism.

Since repacking bearings doesn't rank number one on my list of favorite recreational pursuits, I hustled through the job as quickly as I could and got the wheel back in place.

I was wiping the grease off my hands, when Heidi said, "Daddy, what are you going to do with this little stick?" The "stick" she held up to me was a two-inch piece of metal known as a cotter pin. In my haste, I'd forgotten to put it back on. The mistake could have been a costly one, since the cotter pin is key to holding the wheel on the axle.

I looked at Heidi and got an idea. "Honey, do you know what just happened here?" I asked her. "God just helped me—and He used you to do it."

She looked surprised, so I went on.

"That 'little stick' holds the wheel on the trailer. God saw that I'd left it off, so I believe He helped you to notice it. I think He gave you the idea to ask me about it. If that hadn't happened the wheel could have come off the trailer while we were driving, and we might have had a bad accident. Someone might even have been killed. The Lord used you to help protect our family from something awful!"

A friend with a teenage daughter also had a similar, but less pleasant, opportunity to point out how God was speaking to her child.

During a phone conversation to a business associate, the mother told a lie to cover a mistake she'd made. When the mother hung up, her daughter said, "Mom, I heard what you said on the phone. Did you tell the truth to that man?"

The girl's mother started to cover her tracks with a lofty explanation about "how things are done in the business world." Then she felt the convicting prick of the Holy Spirit, and took a deep breath.

"Honey, I have a confession," she said with embarrassment. "I did lie. And if God hadn't let you hear that conversation, I might have gotten away with it. He's using you to help me see my wrong, so I can get it straightened out."

That may seem too humbling for some parents—but how do our children learn what the voice of God sounds like unless we help them, even if it means admitting we are wrong sometimes? When the Lord spoke to Samuel, the boy thought it was the voice of Eli, the priest (1 Samuel). Eli had to convince him the voice was God's, not his.

In the same way, God speaks to your children and mine continually. But unless we help them to know His voice, they might not respond.

I wanted Heidi to know that God's voice would most likely come to her as a thought. And that she could know the thought was from God because His will was accomplished when she responded to the thought.

David Mains, radio pastor of the Chapel of the Air, calls this process "taking your children on a God hunt." By playing the God Hunt Game with his children, he helps alert them to God speaking to them, and to God at work in and through them. At one point, he gave each of his children a thirty-day calendar on which they were to record some way they saw God at work each day. As the family shared in this God hunt, his children learned how easy it is to see God's involvement in their lives when they know where to look.

Passing on a spiritual legacy sounds like an awesome task, and it is. But I believe God will honor and energize our attempts to help our children find Him for themselves. He is, after all, the One who promised, "You will find [Me] if you look for [Me] with all your heart and with all your soul" (Deuteronomy 4:29b). That applies to our children as well as to us.

12

Letting Go

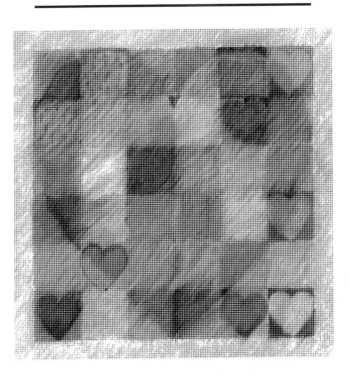

ANNIE: Early in our parenting experience, Steve's mother told us the hardest part of raising kids wasn't the labor and delivery. It wasn't getting up at night with them when they were sick, and it wasn't providing the money for food and other necessities, even though all these things were challenges. The hardest part of parenting for her was letting go.

In our opinion, the struggles of the teen years seem to be God's way of making it easier to let go of our children. (Do I hear an "Amen"?)

Lately, Nathan has begun to wildly wave me out of his room when he's on the phone with a g-i-r-l. Heidi wants to fix her own hair for school, because my styling attempts don't suit her anymore.

I know I should be cheering about these changes. They mean our children are growing toward independence. But during this period of transition, I don't always feel like cheering. Like the day Nathan and I were discussing a difference of opinion and he said, "Mom, you pray for me, and I'll try to make a wise decision about this."

Hold on! I wanted to make the decision, and let him pray for me! That's the way it worked all those years when he was little.

Helping our children grow away from us demands a whole new set of skills. But they're skills I want to acquire, because the alternative sounds bleak, indeed. Listen to this report from Newsweek magazine:

> Sandy and Marvin Miller have three children, ages 19 to 25, and are wondering when they'll grow up. Though the younger two come and go, all three consider their parents' lavish house in Encino, California, home. Each child's bedroom is equipped with a stereo and color TV set. "Our kids were spoiled rotten," Sandy admits.
>
> Jason, the youngest, is enrolled in college. Last summer his parents promised to buy him a Jeep—if he got a job. But Jason "just fooled around," his mother complains, and now Jason is upset because they won't give him the car.
>
> Mia, 22, also attends college. Like her brothers, she has never had to work except for pocket money. The Millers hit the roof, though, when Mia's recent college bill included hundreds of dollars in parking tickets on her Mustang convertible. "She's so used to having us pay for everything, she has absolutely no sense of values," her mother says.
>
> But the real problem is Todd, the oldest child. With a loan from his parents, Todd started a limousine business from the family home. His parents have given him till the year's end to move out and have even offered to lend him the money to buy a house. But Todd refuses to budge. He pays no rent and gets his clothes laundered free by the family

maid. "I grew up here," he argues. "You're throwing me out of my own house."

"I don't want to throw them out in the street," Sandy Miller says of her children. "But they've got to take responsibility and stand on their own two feet. They've got to grow up."[1]

Stories like this get me shaking right down to my Reeboks. When I get too sentimental about "my babies growing up" I remember the alternative and my tears dry right up. So we're listening carefully to those who've successfully launched their children out into adulthood. Here are some of the ideas they've shared with us.

Letting them go starts younger than you think.

Last year Steve decided he wanted to take the kids on a deep-sea fishing excursion 90 miles out in the Gulf of Mexico. This sounded wonderful to me, especially since I'd get six days to myself. I packed up their tennies and a two-gallon jug of sunscreen and sent them off.

It wasn't until they'd left me that I realized what I'd agreed to. My babies were going to be spending three days in a boat bobbing around in the deep, dark waters of the Gulf of Mexico. Wasn't that where they filmed *Jaws*? And didn't I hear last year that a hurricane started there? In fact, wasn't "Gilligan's Island" somewhere on the

---

[1] "Young Beyond Their Years," *Newsweek* Winter/Spring edition 1990, p. 54.

edge of the Gulf of Mexico? I didn't sleep the whole first night.

None of my fears held water. The kids came home with tales of an adventure they'll never forget. And I was a bit smitten, as I thought of a challenge to fathers from the book *Between Parent and Child* by Dr. Hiam Ginott:

> Just as he must defend the mother against an abusive child, so must the father defend the child against an overprotective mother. It is not implied here that all mothers are overprotective. But some mothers enjoy babying their children far beyond infancy. It is the father's function to provide the child with love that is more than merely sheltering, but is liberation as well.[2]

I never mean to baby them, really. I'm just being a mom. Most mothers believe their little birdies need shelter far longer than dads do. Like the mother who complained about her husband, "He expects children barely out of diapers to paint fences, stack wood, rake leaves, shovel snow, hoe cornfields, tote that barge, lift that bale, and to do it all smiling cheerfully while keeping their clothes clean and their shoes in mint condition."[3]

But is this father really such an ogre, or is he simply being a dad instead of a mom?

Most fathers make terrible mothers. When the

---

[2]Dr. Hiam Ginott, *Between Parent and Child* (New York: Avon Books, 1965), pp. 202, 203.
[3]Quoted in "Mommy Wants a Real Job," Sandye Tillrock Voight, *Redbook*, June 1987, p. G–7.

kids were little, and I put them to bed, it was a 45-minute ordeal. We had jammies to match, ears to scrub, stories to read and backs to rub. When Steve put them to bed, he'd look up from the TV show he was watching and bark, "Go to bed." After a day or two of this, of course, the kids would be wearing underwear that could stand alone, and have green fuzz growing on their teeth. When he'd do daytime duty with them, they'd often miss their naps and run around in unmatched outfits.

But our baby birds need to be pushed out of the nest, and this rough-and-tumble element men bring to parenting can be just the thing that provides that needed push. We moms can start the process of letting go by releasing our little ones to their father's care, then allowing him to care for them in the way he sees best.

Letting go means not expecting to center our future on our kids.

Last year in a TV special, the Brady Bunch reunited when Ma and Pa Brady paid for plane tickets to bring all the kids and their spouses back home. It made for a schmaltzy, sentimental journey for this fictitious clan.

A friend of mine watched the show with her teenage daughter. "Honey," she said to her child, "what would you say if, after you leave home, Daddy and I planned to vacation with you and your family every year?"

The girl rolled her eyes. "I'd say, 'Mom, *get a life!*' "

I think the girl showed good sense.

Parents can become too dependent on their grown children, seducing them to stay too close so Mama and Papa have a reason for living. When their nineteen-year-old son wanted to move into his own apartment, one family kept him home with the promise of his own weight room in the basement. Their daughter stayed close because they kept themselves always available when she wanted baby-sitting for her children.

We're not immune from this kind of silliness, and unless we're careful we'll end up in the misery of a child-centered marriage.

Steve and I are determined to keep our marriage strong enough to last when there are only two of us again. Though parenting is an enormously important part of our lives, it is only one part. We help each other remember this by taking time away for just the two of us. It may be going out to dinner, or a night away at a hotel, or an evening out with other couples. Being away from the kids helps us focus on each other, and reminds us we're more than just Heidi's dad or Nathan's mom. We're individuals, and we're a couple. We were alone before the kids came, and we will be again.

We work, too, at making plans for life after the kids leave home, and Heidi and Nathan know it. We want them to feel free to leave, without harboring guilt pangs that their departure has left us moping and sighing the lonely nights away wondering when the kids are going to call.

With these thoughts in mind, Steve wrote this song:

> Children, please give me your kind attention,
> I've something to say; here's my intention—
> I'm gonna go out with your mother tonight,
> And no you can't come; it won't help if you
>   cry.
> Now, you may wonder how I could be
> So heartless to want just your mother and me.
> Well, she's your dear mother, I know that it's
>   true,
> But she was my sweetheart before there was
>   you.
> First, we'll walk by the ocean and we're gonna
>   hold hands,
> And we'll write our names in the wet sand.
> We'll write "I love you's," send them off in a
>   bottle.
> And in memory of you, we'll eat at Mc-
>   Donald's.
> Oh, you may wonder, how I could be
> So heartless to want just your mother and me.
> Well, she's your dear mother, I know that it's
>   true,
> But she was my sweetheart before there was
>   you.[4]

Your kids have to release you, too.

Steve grew up in a church where the wearing of jewelry was strictly forbidden. They took literally and strictly the scriptural admonition that says, "Your beauty should not come from out-

---

[4]"Before There Was You," Times and Seasons Music. Used by permission.

ward adornment, such as the wearing of gold jewelry."

When we got married, Steve didn't wear a wedding ring.

Actually, he did wear a ring, but only when he wasn't around his parents. His understanding of Scripture had changed since his youth, and by the time we married he no longer believed God forbade all Christians to wear jewelry.

But his parents still held to this conviction, so whenever we'd go home to West Virginia the wedding ring would come off.

It wasn't so much that Steve feared their disapproval, or was tied to his mother's apron strings. Rather, he respected them so much he didn't want to hurt them. And I admired his sensitivity, so I didn't pressure him.

Finally there came a time when Steve got caught in his duplicity. We had a photo taken for a new album cover, and there was Steve's wedding band in the picture, shining for all the world to see. The jig was up. Either he'd have to tell his parents the truth, or we'd have to reshoot the album cover.

As it turned out, his parents were less disappointed by Steve's jewelry than they were by the fact that he'd not told them earlier. To them the wearing of jewelry wasn't the major issue Steve had expected it would be.

But telling them did something liberating for Steve. His parents had let go of him, but he needed to let go of them, as well. Differing with them about the wearing of jewelry was what it took for him to release them, and to give up a childish need for their approval.

We need to let go of our children, but they also need to learn to let go of us. For them to mature, we'll need to become less their authority and more their counselor and friend. Later, as we grow old, they may even see the need to parent us. These necessary changes will take place more gracefully if we both let go.

Release is hardest when the kids don't turn out as you had hoped they would.

I don't know if life holds a pain deeper than that felt by parents whose children have strayed. A mother whose beautiful, gifted daughter ran away from home said, "It's worse than if she had died. At least then we'd have been left with happy memories of our years together. Now those memories mock us. Sometimes we're furious at her for hurting us so deeply. At other times we're overcome with guilt as we agonize over what we must have done wrong to make her turn out like this."

Looking into the eyes of these wounded parents makes me wonder how long we are to be responsible for our kids' behavior. I've heard parenting experts say that children are wet cement, so the responsibility for what they become as adults depends entirely on how that cement was shaped by their parents. I used to agree, but lately I'm taking a second look at scriptural admonitions to parents.

Surely no one could have enjoyed more perfect parenting than did Adam, yet he chose to stray from the right path. And Jesus was surely the perfect leader for the twelve disciples. Yet one of them betrayed Him to death.

We're responsible to offer our children a godly heritage and to teach them how to be good stewards of it. But we can't force them to do the right thing with the inheritance we've given them.

Jesus' parable of the prodigal son bears this out. In this story, the father loved both his boys, yet one chose to live responsibly while the other squandered his inheritance in frivolous living. Though the father's heart was surely broken he didn't lock his wayward son in the basement to keep him from leaving home. But neither did he run to the far country to bail the boy out when his foolishness sent him to the pigpens. He let the boy hit bottom, and after he did, the journey home began.

If your children have strayed, it is right that you listen to them, and search your own heart for ways you might have wronged them. We've already had to ask our children to forgive us for times we've intentionally or unintentionally wounded them.

If they forgive you, receive it. But even if they don't, you need to seek God's forgiveness, and then forgive yourself. As God releases you from guilt—both real and false—you will be freer to release your children to live out the consequences of their choices, and perhaps to find their way back home.

We need to let God
loose in our children's lives.

When our children are small, most of our work with them has to do with setting boundaries. "Don't do this . . . do that." But there comes a time when we not only have to stop telling our kids what to do, but we also have to stop telling God what to do with them, for them, and to them.

We have to let them go on the winds of His Spirit, which may allow them to be carried in directions we wouldn't choose. When these directions frighten us, we can pray against them, but we may find ourselves praying *against* God. Better still, we can seek to get on a new wave-length with God by praising Him for the work His Spirit is doing, even when His molding seems to be done with a welder's torch, rather than the delicate artist's brush we'd prefer.

When we let God loose in our children's lives, and commit ourselves to prayer in cooperation with Him, He finds ways to work we couldn't design or dream of. Steve's mother used to pray, "Whatever it takes to bring Steve back to You, do it." We take courage from one of God's answers to that particular prayer.

Steve was stationed in Spain, and one night he'd gone with his buddies to a bowling alley. As he took a table in the lounge, first drink in hand, intending not to walk out sober, he looked across the room and there sat Beau Meadows, a boy from Steve's high school!

Steve was mortified. Beau had been there

when Steve won the "Most Religious" award (believe it or not). He'd heard Steve give daily devotions over the school intercom, and he knew all about Steve's heritage as a preacher's son. Now he'd caught the preacher's son redhanded, doing what he knew was wrong.

To make matters worse, Beau recognized Steve at once and came over to say hello. Steve turned bright red, and with eyes downcast, mumbled some embarrassed small-talk. Then he made a feeble excuse to end the conversation. He left the tavern with the warning beating in his brain, "Be sure your sins will find you out," and with the conviction of his sin hanging heavy on his heart.

It was no coincidence that Beau Meadows showed up in that Spanish tavern. Even though Steve had turned away from God, the Lord was still seeking him. And He continued to pursue him until Steve came back to Christ. I believe He does this for all the children of praying parents.

We've drawn courage from the experience of best-selling author Catherine Marshall who agonized over the rebellion of her stepdaughter Linda.

Their conflicts started over minor issues, like differences in choice of clothes. When Linda reached high school, they fought over her disappointing academic performance. Nearly every report card carried teachers' comments about "poor attitude and motivation." Tutors and a prep school made no difference.

Things got worse when Linda went to college,

and picked up the dress and rebellious lifestyle of the '60s.

Catherine Marshall reflected, "Most of us parents with children caught up in all this know the feeling . . . wondering whether our sons and daughters might be ensnared in experiences dark enough that we would prefer not to know specifics. Especially when they were away from home, we told ourselves that 'what we don't know won't hurt us,' meanwhile knowing full well that the ostrich never solves anything with his head in the sand."

But after Linda's graduation weekend, Catherine Marshall came away with such a heavy spirit she knew there would be no peace without letting go of her resentments toward Linda for the pain she'd inflicted on her. The list of offenses filled three pages, but as she wrote them, she relinquished her right to judge her stepdaughter, and released her to God's bidding.

In Linda's case, changes followed quickly. As is usually so, people other than her parents were the catalysts to begin the change. Later, Linda experienced a pivotal moment one afternoon as she prepared to take a shower. As she stood with one foot on the bathroom rug and the other in the shower stall, it came to her that one foot in and one out accurately depicted her life. She'd made commitments to God, yet lived in rebellion against Him. It was time to choose.

She said, "Standing there, I carefully weighed what choosing the Lord's side would cost me. Obviously, some things in my life would have to go.

But I was tired of living in two worlds and not enjoying either. I longed desperately for His peace in my heart. I took a deep breath and said aloud, 'I choose you, Lord.' Then I got in the shower. That shower was my true baptism."

In the days ahead, Linda and her parents talked and confessed and cried and forgave. Linda released her hostility and guilt; her parents owned up to mistakes and fears and a lack of understanding.

A new life began for Linda. She sought spiritual help, and moved on to minister with a Christian fellowship in Washington, D.C.[5] Today, she is a lovely Christian mother of two, raising her own children to love and serve the Lord.

As Christian parents, we need to remember it's like the man says, "It ain't over, till it's over." Both Steve and Catherine Marshall's stepdaughter represent the multitudes of children who seemed to abandon the God of their father, only to come back to Him with greater fervor than they ever had before, and to follow Him in ways their parents wouldn't have dreamed.

It is never too early or too late to release your children to Him, determining to trust Him to make of their lives that which He intends.

When we *let them go* into the Lord's hands, it is then we present to our children the best gift of all—a God and Father whose love and care for them will never end.

---

[5]Catherine Marshall, *Something More* (New York: McGraw-Hill, 1974), pp. 45–51.

For those interested in receiving our newsletter, learning more about our music ministry, or for concert information please write:

HARMONY FOR THE HOME
P.O. Box 41275
Nashville, TN 37204